LEADING ON THE

CREATIVE EDGE

Gaining Competitive Advantage Through the Power of Creative Problem Solving

ROGER L. FIRESTIEN, PhD

Executive Forum
2012

Library of Congress Catalog Card Number:96-17575
ISBN 18917-41020

Cover illustration: Shane Ewald/Studio47

Some of the anecdotal illustrations in this book are true to life and are included with the permission of the persons involved. All other illustrations are composites of real situations, and any resemblances to people living or dead is coincidental.

This publication is designed to provide accurate and authoritative information in regard to the subject matter covered. It is sold with the understanding that the author and publisher are not engaged in rendering legal, accounting, or other professional service. If legal advise or other expert assistance is required, the services of a competent professional person should be sought. *From a Declaration of Principles jointly adopted by a Committe of the American Bar Association and a Committe of Publishers.*

Firestien, Roger L., 1995-
    Leading on the creative edge : gaining competitive advantage through the power of creative problem solving / Roger L. Firestien.
        p.   cm.
    ISBN 1-89174-102-0(softcover)
    1.Creative ability in business. 2.Problem solving. 3. Leadership.
    I. Title.
    HD53.F568 1996
    658.4'03 — dc20
                                                            96-17575
                                                            CIP

Printed in the United States of America
1 2 3 4 5 6 7 8 9 10/99 98 97 96

Contents

—❖—

To my daughter, Maria,
may your beautiful, creative spirit always shine

To the memory of my dad,
Wilbert 'Chuck' Firestien and

To the memory of my grandfather,
George Brug, Jr.

Acknowledgments

Acts of creation, like writing books, developing a new product, or founding a company involve many people. I owe my deepest gratitude and heartfelt thanks to the following people.

Steve Halliday, for his patience, understanding, and extraordinary writing skills that transformed a rough meandering manuscript into a book that sings.

Traci Mullins, formerly the senior editor at Piñon Press, who saw the potential in this work and encouraged me to write this book.

Lois Donovan, my company's executive assistant, who toiled over rambling transcriptions of interviews and kept the company running while I "hid out" and wrote this book. Lois, I couldn't have done this without you.

Gary Gorski, our company's computer whiz, technical expert, and the man who "makes stuff work around here". Thank you for your steadfast caring and friendship over the past 23 years.

Carol Anderson, for her caring support and insights into many of the organizational applications of creativity in this book.

Jonathan Vehar, for his wit, loving sarcasm, and for asking tough questions that continually challenge my thinking about creativity.

Blair Miller, for his friendship and work on making Creative Problem Solving more accessible to the "whole person."

Diane Foucar-Szocki and Bill Shephard, for their love, friendship, and pioneering work in the field of Creative Problem Solving.

Tracey Jung and Jerome Mach, for their understanding of the creative process that help sustain me through the tough times with this book.

Ken Kumiega, for his powerful organizational insights that helped provide a foundation for the book.

Chris Grivas, for his research ability to sleuth out some of the difficult and obscure references.

Dave Meier, for being a model of an organizational leader who inspires and nurtures creativity.

Robert Eckert, for his powerful insights into the brain/body/spirit connection.

Shane Ewald, who took my scribbles and turned them into the clear diagrams that led to the wonderful graphics for this book.

Gerard Puccio, for your extraordinary leadership at the International Center for Studies in Creativity and the gentle way you advance the commmunity of creativity.

Mary Murdock, for her insights on the creative person and the importance of falling in love with a vision for the future.

Sid Parnes and Ruth Noller, for their inspiration and giving their gifts of creativity to so many people around the world.

Goran Ekvall and Teresa Amabile, for their pioneering work on the climate that nurtures the creativity in organizations.

Janet DiClaudio, Bill Royster, Peter Pellegrino, Dave Newcomer, Jeff Harris, Peter Grazer, Nathan Bliss, Perry Buffington, Robb LaBranche, Greg McGlone, and Joel Goodman, for allowing me to interview you and share your stories of the courageous application of Creative Problem Solving you have made in your organizations.

Ruth and Chuck Firestien, my mom and dad, who made my world a safe place to express my creativity as I was growing up. Thanks for helping me make go-carts out of worn-out wagons, tree houses out of wood scraps, rafts out of old oil drums. Thanks for helping me with my 4-H projects, teaching me how to take and develop my own pictures, listening to my deafening rock band practice in the basement, and for not yelling too loudly when I stunk up the house with my chemistry experiments.

Winning in the Marketplace

If you are a corporate executive, manager, supervisor, teacher, college professor, minister, doctor, coach, volunteer, or even a parent who wants to unleash the creativity of the people you lead, then this is your book.

I assume you are like most of the leaders I have worked with over the last several years. Face it. Your competition likely has the same product, technology and delivery system that you do. You are facing tremendous change and heated competition, whether you are rushing to get your latest product to market or trying to attract more members to your church.

Beyond that, it's quite possible you're facing cutbacks or down-sizing, or you're still smarting from the last round of re-engineering and reinvention. Still ringing in your ears are the demands to "do more with less" and "work smarter, not harder." No doubt you've tried solutions that used to work-but those solutions just aren't enough anymore; the problems (or what you think are the problems) have changed.

The fact is, *the only competitive edge you have is how you harness the creative energies of the people who work with and for you to develop new approaches to problems and implement solutions that work.* Creative Problem Solving has never been more important than today.

But how do you work smarter? How do you do more with less? How do you create new approaches and creative solutions to difficult problems?

This book will deliver practical methods you can immediately apply to help you become more creative and to nurture the creativity in the people who work for you. Result?

Competitive advantage that makes you a winner in the marketplace.

Think of this book as an instruction manual that will help you to lead on the creative edge. I will lay out a process that will enable you to redefine problems so that they can be solved more effectively, generate more ideas than you ever thought possible, and build and implement ideas to create worthwhile change or improvement. All of this will occur with a focus on you, the leader, and the crucial role that you play in guiding your organization toward the future.

This procedure is called Creative Problem Solving, and it has helped hundreds of businesses over the past four decades to gain the competitive advantage they need to win in the marketplace. Creative Problem Solving has been applied successfully in scores of situations, including automobile manufacturing, hospitals, churches, schools, high-tech companies, government agencies, product packaging design, paper manufacturing, large organizational computer systems, and even fertilizer manufacturing.

The value of using a specific process for creativity is that it provides you with a blueprint or a method for problem solving. When you have a problem solving method that works, you can more effectively solve problems. This approach is much more efficient than trying to decide how you are going to attack a problem when it crosses your path. By knowing the system, you can focus on *what* you might do to solve the problem instead of wasting time trying to decide *how* you are going to solve the problem. A structured process for creativity helps you to work the problem more efficiently.

Within these pages you will meet leaders from a variety of organizations who have implemented Creative Problem Solving methodologies in their organizations. You will learn of the challenges and successes these leaders have faced and enjoyed as they attempted to make their organizations more creative places. When you're finished with this book, you should clearly understand the critical role a leader plays in fostering creativity in an organization and how that creativity leads directly to bottom-line financial success. But most importantly, it will give you skills to help you achieve that success.

Because this book focuses on solutions, you will discover it is not a collection of 1001 idea-generating techniques. It does not focus on gimmicky games you must play to be "creative" You won't be told you must memorize truckloads of creativity jargon and acronyms in order to be creative. This book is not a technical dissection of the creative process or a collection of leadership principles and theories. It is not a book on how to negotiate the best deal, resolve a union strike, discipline an employee, fire someone or become a debt-free millionaire.

It *is* a book that will introduce you to seven of the most effective creativity principles I have used over the last twenty-four years. Each principle will be developed in two chapters: the first will lay a theoretical foundation, the second will build on and apply that foundation. The goal all along is to help you achieve significant, even startling, results. I will introduce you to some all-purpose creativity tools that will be effective on just about any problem or challenge you might encounter. All of the methods I will present have been scientifically validated in a number of settings. This stuff *works!*

Bottom line? This book focuses on *results.* Creativity for creativity's sake is great (and it can be a lot of fun), but in today's world we need to achieve significant results at a much faster pace than at any other time in history. Therefore, I will provide you with specific actions designed to nurture your own creativity and to help the people who work with you to focus their creative ability in such a way that organizational and personal performance will dramatically improve.

BUT DOES THIS APPLY TO ME?

At this point I predict someone might be saying, "Well, that's good. But I didn't see my organization in your list. My business is different. I don't think this stuff applies to me."

Don't be so sure!

Often, when I am negotiating a contract with an organization-whether the company wants me to deliver a speech, lead a multiple-day Creative Problem Solving training program, facilitate a Creative Problem Solving session, guide some strategic planning, or help with new product development the client makes a point to tell me just how different her business is from any other business I have ever worked with. And yes, her organization is different . . . but only about ten percent different.

Over the course of my career I have found that organizations are about 90 percent the same and about ten percent different. The 90 percent of similarity derives from the fact that all organizations are comprised of a group of people who (it is hoped) are working together toward a common goal. I emphasize "it is hoped" because many times people are *not* working toward a common goal. Many times they don't even know what the goal is. The 10 percent of difference focuses on the specific product or service that the organization delivers. That 10 percent is the difference between getting more people to join a church or manufacturing transmission gears for cars.

The good news is that the creativity methods you will learn in this book are designed to work in *any* type of organization. They are designed to help people renew their creative ability and focus their ideas for action, regardless of their sphere of work. My ultimate goal is to show you how creativity can be a strategic business weapon crucial to gaining a competitive edge in the marketplace. Of course, we'll have a little fun along the way, but we can't afford to lose sight of the book's central theme:
Creative Problem Solving can make your business a clear winner.

So let's get on the winning track right now!

ONE

The Key to Your Company's Success

*The greatest threat to any organization is not the lack of ability
or resources, but the failure of imagination.*
DAVID MEIER, DIRECTOR,
Center for Accelerated Learning

Creativity is a strategic business weapon. The organizations
that will survive and thrive in the twenty-first century will not
be the ones with the deepest pockets, but the ones that can
unleash and apply the creativity of their workforce. And the
organizations that will do this best are the ones with leaders
who recognize and take steps to promote such creativity.

Without question, the key to a company's creativity (or
lack of it) is its leaders. According to Goran Ekvall of the
University of Lund, Sweden,

> Sixty-seven percent of the statistical variance accounted
> for on the climate for creativity in organizations is direct-
> ly attributed to the behavior of the leader.[1]

In other words, if things are going well in your organization — if people are invested in their work, if they are contributing ideas and successfully moving initiatives forward and
think your organization is a great place to work-there is a 67
percent chance that you are doing some things right.
On the other hand, if your people are not involved in the life of
the organization, if they loathe their jobs and think your company is a wretched place to work, there is a 67 percent chance
that it is your fault.

Leader, the cold, hard truth is that your behavior is the
single most important factor in determining whether the peo-

ple who work for you will be creative. Creativity is not best produced by open offices, beautiful views of corporate parks,
tremendous amounts of capital resources, the best distribu-
tion system, or the best product in the world. None of this
makes a bit of difference if you do not support your people in
developing their ideas and implementing new approaches for
solving problems. In fact, only one corporate future is likely for
the company that fails to develop such new ideas or approaches to solving problems: obsolescence and eventual collapse.

If you think such a prediction is overly gloomy, consider
some startling statistics. It turns out such a dark future is far
easier to create than most of us would like to imagine.

According to a recent study reported in *Brandweek*
magazine, the odds of creating a breakthrough product idea
that will meet a company's marketplace objectives are a pitiful
one in 100. The study found that only 39 percent of product
proposals actually begin the development process; 17 percent
of those proposals complete the process; a slight 8 percent are
eventually introduced to the market; and a tiny 1 percent ever
go on to meet stated objectives. This translates into a "waste
rate" of 99 percent![2]

WHAT IS CREATIVITY?

If we are going to foster creativity, we need to know what creativity is. We need to know what creativity skills are before
we can develop them.

So, what is creativity?

There have been many attempts to define creativity. In
1961 a researcher named Mel Rhodes set out to find the single unifying definition of creativity. He couldn't do it, and
that's probably a good thing. Otherwise, we would continually judge ourselves against one definition. From the forty definitions of creativity that he found in 1961, Rhodes saw about
four clusters.

One cluster of definitions centered on what a creative
person was. What's a creative personality like? Psychologists
who were working to identify geniuses and eminent personal-
ities had a lot to say about the creative personality. Many of
the early studies on leadership that attempted to list the
traits or characteristics of the ideal leader were in the "person" category. continued on page 15

continued from page 14

A second cluster of definitions described a creative *process*. What are the means by which people develop new ideas and put those ideas into action? People like Alex Osborn (the advertising executive who invented brainstorming and was the "O" in the advertising agency BBD&O) were doing a lot of work in the area of creative process.

A third group of definitions focused on a creative *product*. How do you know if something is creative? How do you know if art is true or beautiful? How do you know if a product is going to sell?

The final batch of definitions emphasized the *press*-that is, the environment in which people feel most likely to contribute their ideas, get involved in the life of the organization, and make the organization's initiatives their own. The press is where leaders have the most influence in nurturing or destroying the creativity of those who work for them.

In 1987 Scott Isaksen, developed the following diagram to represent how these four "Ps" of creativity interact with one another. It's one way to understand creativity.

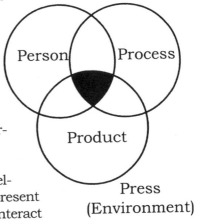

Person   Process

Product

Press
(Environment)

Why such a high product mortality rate? Is it the competition, the economy, a failure of creativity, a shortage of ideas? No. The shocking answer is: It's the boss's fault.

According to a recent Innovation Survey from Group EFO, Ltd. of Weston, Connecticut, 63 percent of new product marketers say top management at their companies does not have a clear strategic vision of the role of new products. Another 65 percent say top management does not make a significant contribution to finished product concepts. Yet that isn't the worst news: a full 35 percent wishes top management was less involved than it is![3]

The question is, why? One new product manager spoke for many when he said, "My management's motto is test, retest and retest. The focus seems to be to find three reasons not to pursue an idea rather than to figure how best to do it"[4]

Sadly, this seems to be the rule rather than the exception and there are many reasons why senior management handles new product ideas so negatively. Sometimes leaders have been promoted through other departments and so lack a basic grasp of the concepts involved. Often they simply don't know the right terms. In other cases senior managers have not been taught to deal effectively with new concepts. They have built their entire careers on quick judgments and quarterly returns; they have been taught to evaluate an idea carefully by pointing out all its flaws . . . and as a result they never help their product managers overcome the problems that inevitably plague new projects. Managers also may fail to look carefully at the strengths or potential in the new ideas.

By the way, this explains why most new products are merely line extensions. By evaluating ideas negatively and by failing to look at the potential in a new concept, companies get very good at making better versions of someone else's initiative. The catch is that the consumer views these products as nothing more than "me too" efforts, and so the product languishes.

WHAT IS CREATIVITY? (PART TWO)

Some people like to distinguish between creativity and innovation. Some say that creativity is getting the idea, while innovation is doing something about it.

But one definition I like is very simple: *Creativity is novelty that is useful.* I like this definition because it expresses the tension that occurs when we talk about creativity. Most of us agree that a "creative" thing must be new or unique or novel. But the solution also has to *work.* The solution has to solve a problem, even if it is solving a problem only for the creator of the idea. So one working definition for creativity is this: Novelty that is useful.[5]

It simply can't be stressed too much or too often: *The behavior of the leader is the single most important factor in determining whether the people who work for him will be creative.* And when workers are encouraged to be creative, companies reap the substantial benefits. Consider the following examples:

✶ To create a culture that fosters teamwork and innovation, employees at Mazda were trained in Creative Problem Solving, teambuilding, and continuous improvement. The result: Employees met productivity and quality levels days ahead of schedule. In fact, supervisors report that employees trained in creativity came up to speed *two weeks* faster than their untrained counterparts.

✶ During a training session in Creative Problem Solving, employees at a General Motors forge plant in upstate New York set their sights on finding a way to prevent the ring gears made at their plant from sticking in and breaking dies during production – a problem that was costing the plant thousands of dollars each week. While brainstorming, one teammate suggested using the cooking product PAM to prevent the sticking, and another participant quickly built on the idea. The result: Using a $1.00 spray bottle and fifty cents worth of non-stick solutions, plant operators now spray the dies to prevent sticking, and the plant saves as much as $40,000 weekly (see chapter 6).

✶ When first asked by a key customer to supply paper that was 95 percent bright, Mead replied, "We simply can't do it." In fact, Mead struggled for years to enhance the brightness of its papers without success. Invigorated by a creativity workshop, however, Mead assembled a team to tackle the problem. The result: The team improved the brightness of Mead's paper, developed a new world-class line of products superior to any of Mead's competitors, and developed a new process that saves more than half a million dollars each year (see chapter 6).

A recent survey by Yankelovich Partners Inc., published by *Business Week*, indicates that workers themselves believe there's a lot of room to increase company profits, even beyond the greater productivity that has characterized American work practices over the past decade.[6] Although 70 percent of the 1,200 workers interviewed said they were happy in their current jobs, 86 percent felt they could still boost productivity by an average of 26 percent, given the right incentives and conditions. The biggest barriers to higher productivity? Inadequate supervision and employee involvement in decision-making; too much work; and insufficient rewards and chances to advance.

Of course, it takes creativity to develop and implement the incentives and conditions that would foster such increased productivity. It simply is not obvious how to stimulate such marked increases; if it were, every company would do it.

But *how* do you stimulate such creativity in your organization? I know of many organizations which continue to spend millions of dollars creating beautiful places to work, expecting that when the staff moves into some shiny new building they will be magically transformed into creative giants. When the expected metamorphosis doesn't take place, they're surprised and disappointed. My question is, why? Why are they surprised when they spend almost nothing to train their managers and supervisors on the behaviors they will need to lead their people to find solutions to tough problems?

The uncomfortable yet unsurprising truth is that most of us find it easier to build a multi-million dollar building than to change the way we think. And the way we have been taught to think, act, and lead is the biggest deterrent to becoming more creative.

DOES TWO PLUS TWO EVER EQUAL FIVE?
From elementary school through college, we were taught there was but one right answer to a problem. Two plus two always equals four. We also learned that the quicker we got the right answer, the "smarter" we were.

This quick solution syndrome continued as we began our professional lives. We learned that the sign of a successful leader is decisiveness; she always has the right answer. I recall one leader telling me, "I make decisions, lots of them. I make a lot of wrong decisions, but I always make a decision."
Even I, a person who has been in the creativity business for over twenty years, still need to remind myself of such basics as:

> ∗ Looking at problems as situations that can be resolved rather than as insurmountable obstacles
> ∗ Deferring judgment

✱Looking for the strengths in an idea first

And so on.

Think about it. If our creativity wasn't trained out of us by an educational system that has traditionally focused on our weaknesses rather than our strengths; if we weren't taught that the way to climb the out-dated corporate ladder was to compete with each other instead of cooperate with each other; if we weren't taught that there is only one right answer to a problem and the quicker you get that answer, the smarter you are; if we weren't taught that having a problem to solve was an indication that we were wrong or weak; if we weren't taught that asking questions is a sign of incompetence-then you wouldn't be reading this book and I wouldn't have a job, because we would all be naturally creative. We would be naturally creative just the way we were when we were children. We wouldn't be afraid to take a fresh look at the problems that confront us.

That is why it is so important to wake up and consciously change our behavior; to consciously take a look at how our actions affect the people who work in our organizations.

Carol Anderson, Research Scientist at The Procter and Gamble company, advises us to "Be aware of everything that is going on around you—up, down, behind you, all over. Listen not only to what is said but also to what is not said. Notice what is done and what is not done. Insights come from what is not said and what is not done."[7]

AS NATURAL AS A HEARTBEAT

There is nothing mysterious about the creative process. It is a natural process, as natural as breathing or your heartbeat. Nature seems to operate under two basic principles: *divergence* and *convergence*. When nature diverges, it generates thousands of unique combinations of plant and animal life. Then, through the process of natural selection, it converges and chooses for survival the most adaptable species.

To be more creative, we can take a lesson from nature. When working to solve a problem or capitalize on an opportunity, first, diverge. continued on page 20

continued from page 19

Stretch your thinking and generate many options. Only after that should you converge and select the best of those options to refine and put into action.

It's not hard to remember: diverge, then converge. You might say that diverging and converging is, in fact, the heartbeat of the creative process.

To change our thinking and then to change our behavior requires that we take an honest look at ourselves. When I force myself to honestly look in the mirror, I often find things that I really don't want to see. I see that I've been wrong. I see that I've made mistakes. I see that I've hurt people who were important to me. Admitting these mistakes makes me vulnerable and very uncomfortable, yet it's crucial if I want to move ahead and succeed in areas where I've failed before.

One of the biggest errors that many of us make is to stubbornly believe that we are not creative. We must deal with that misconception at the beginning, or we can get nowhere.

WE ARE ALL CREATIVE . . . EVEN LEADERS

Take a walk with me for a moment down the corridor of a major metropolitan art gallery. Look around. We pass paintings by Cezanne, Renoir, Gauguin and Van Gogh. There is no doubt that our society recognizes these as creative works. As we look at these paintings, most of us don't believe we could create something so treasured. Most of us don't think of ourselves as creative. Most of us believe that only artists, composers, and inventors can be creative.

But that's utterly untrue. Research has found that we are all creative and we all express our creativity in different and valuable ways. As a matter of fact, our creativity can be enhanced deliberately.

CREATIVITY STYLES

Michael Kirton, a researcher in the United Kingdom, has developed a theory that identifies two types of creativity: *adaptive* creativity and *innovative* creativity. A major part of this theory focuses on how much structure a person prefers to have around the problems on which they work.

continued on page 21

continued from page 20

Any guess as to what type of creativity the Wright Flyer represented? You got it-innovative. Yes, man can fly. The airplane broke the traditional view of the world that was held at that time. However, it was adaptive creativity that improved the airplane to make it more comfortable, safer, and commercially viable. Innovative creativity came up with the facsimile and video technology but it was adaptive creativity that brought this technology to market and made it profitable.

Kirton's theory originated by identifying individuals in organizations who naturally expressed innovative creativity or adaptive creativity. He found that some people were excellent at coming up with ideas to improve the current system, while others were good at creating ideas that challenged or changed the system. Adaptors also accepted the problem that was given to them, while innovators often challenged the established view of the situation.

When these two types of people work together effectively to solve problems, the results can be astounding. However, as you might have guessed, these people see the world very differently. Without an understanding of the natural strengths they use to solve problems, the result can often be war instead of effective problem solving. Kirton's personality assessment, the Kirton Adaption Innovation Inventory, is a helpful tool for members of work teams to complete to gain an understanding of the strengths they bring to a group. Actually, there are very few pure innovators or pure adaptors. Most of us have a mix of innovative and adaptive behaviors. However, we also have a preference for the kinds of ideas we will generate and the kinds of problems we will attempt to solve.

Both types of creativity are important. It is crucial for organizations to support innovative breakthroughs, but it is also important to nurture the patient, long-view, adaptive creativity that is necessary to make breakthroughs commercially viable. People naturally express their creativity in different ways. Businesses need both innovative and adaptive creativity to be successful in the long run.

The classic "Creative Studies Project," completed in 1972 at the Center for Studies in Creativity at the State

University College in Buffalo, New York, found that students who completed a two-year program in creativity and innovation performed significantly better than comparable control students in coping with real-life situational tests, in special English tests, and in math courses. Most students also reported large gains in their own productive, creative behavior, as well as their ability to cope with day-to-day problems. Their creativity couldn't help spilling over into vast areas of their lives!

Abraham Maslow, the eminent psychologist, stressed that a first-rate soup is better than a fourth-rate painting.[8] In other words, the medium in which you choose to create doesn't matter. The important thing is that you express your creativity in some way that is rewarding to you-and, it is hoped, to others.

Most leaders don't work with oil paint, clay, or water colors. They create with the most complex medium of all-people. My artist friends may take exception to my next comment, but artists have it easy. Paint and clay don't go on strike. Paint and clay don't stomp away in anger. Paint and clay can be "told" what to do and always respond without complaining. Paint and clay never need benefit plans, drug abuse counseling, or days off. People are so much more complicated than inanimate media. It takes tremendous effort and dedication to create with people-but the dividends can be phenomenal.

Do you want to help your people achieve extraordinary results and thereby enable your company to enjoy extraordinary success? If so, it's well within your grasp. You simply need to tap the creative person that's inside you.

IMPROVE YOURSELF

A story from ancient China illustrates the attitude today's leaders must take if they wish to lead their organizations to success in the marketplace:

> When Yen Ho was about to take up his duties as tutor to the heir of Ling, Duke of Wei, he went to Ch'u Po Yu for advice.
>
> "I have to deal," he said, "with a man of depraved and murderous disposition.... How is one to deal with a

man of this sort?"

"I am glad," said Ch'u Po Yu, "that you have asked this question. The first thing you must do is not to improve him, but to improve yourself."[9]

Leaders must take personal responsibility for their own creativity. Whether you are the CEO or a manager who reports to someone else, *you* make the difference between an organization that is going to be on the cutting edge, and a me-too outfit. Not only are you responsible for your own creativity, but you must serve as a model for the people who work with and for you. It is vital that you establish an environment that nurtures creativity in your organization. Let your people see you struggle with your own creative ideas and give them the space to develop their own.

Often at breaks in my Creative Problem Solving (CPS) seminars, participants will come up to me and say, "This is great! But you know who really should have heard this? My manager. It is my manager who prevents me from being creative."

Yes, managers do have a powerful influence on a subordinate's creativity — but not all of the influence. Whatever your position, you still have at least a 33 percent chance of doing some creative work even if your manger is Darth Vader's cousin.

As I interviewed people who were using Creative Problem Solving in their organizations, it became clear that most were not at the top of the corporate ladder. Most didn't have an ideal environment to work in, but they did take personal responsibility for their own creativity. As a result, they served as models and nurtured creativity in the people who worked with them.

There is no question that some environments and systems are more conducive to creativity than others. Yet the people who were successful in even less-than-ideal situations had one thing in common: They took personal responsibility for their creativity and made a big difference in the profitability of their companies or divisions.

If IT AIN'T BROKE, DON'T FIX IT

As I conclude this chapter, let me lay to rest one misgiving that might be troubling you. In this book I am not saying that you and your people must be creative all the time. If you have systems or procedures that are working extremely well, then leave them alone. There are times to be creative and times to follow the routine.

I fly on airplanes a lot. If the pilot is coming in for a routine landing at a major metropolitan airport, I don't want him and the co-pilot brainstorming all the ways they might land the plane. I never want to hear the following conversation:

> "Let's see. We could land upside down."
> "We could buzz the control tower."
> "We could see how close we could get to those other nice jets."
> "What if we just had some fun and landed at a different airport? Do you think the passengers would know the difference?"

But if a problem came up that this crew had never encountered and had no procedure for solving, then I would definitely want them to come up with some new solutions. My very survival would depend on their being creative.

The approach to Creative Problem Solving laid out in this book is designed for those situations that are complex and ambiguous, for those circumstances in which you don't have a workable solution and for which you need some imaginative ideas.

Because your role as leader is so crucial and demanding, in the next chapter I will introduce you to specific methods to nurture your own creativity. This is critical, for how can you expect your people to use their creativity to attain results if you are not working to develop your own creativity?

Remember, creativity is not something mysterious or a thing possessed only by a few gifted people. We are all creative and we can all create in different ways. Leaders create with the most complicated and sophisticated medium of all-people, working in an organization to achieve worthwhile goals and objectives. As the lead creator in the organization, it is your role to model and support creativity. Leaders must be congruent. In other words, if you want the people in your organization to be creative, you must also be creative. And as a leader, you must show how you struggle with the new ideas that cross your path. By demonstrating your willingness to try new things and to be flexible, you encourage others to take risks-creative risks that may well take your organization to the top.

And believe me, the view at the summit can be spectacular.

Fly the Fruitful Skies

Changing things is central to leadership,
and changing them before anybody else is creativeness.
ANTHONY JAY

One big reason why organizations are having such a difficult time transforming themselves is that leaders are having a difficult time transforming themselves. Unfortunately, after many years of work, they begin to believe in their own infallibility. After all, they have won the election, climbed to the top of the corporate ladder, written the best-selling books. They are the experts.

As a result, many leaders become excessively defensive and arrogant. They won't tolerate an idea that doesn't fit their world view. Hey, if it was such a good idea, they would have thought of it themselves.

But by slipping into such a mindset, they forget that the expert of today is the dinosaur of tomorrow. To become successful leaders today who will continue to be successful tomorrow, we must become beginners once again. We must always be growing and learning. We can learn something from everybody. According to Dave Meier, "Everyone is our teacher and we are everyone's learning coach."

So how do you begin again? How do you, with all of your vast and valuable knowledge, invoke the child within to see the world with a fresh pair of eyes? In this chapter, we will explore twelve ways to nurture your creativity as a leader so that you can nurture it in the people who work with you.

TWELVE WAYS TO NURTURE YOUR CREATIVITY

One: Develop Creativity Habits

Clasp your hands in front of you. Which thumb is on top, your right or your left? Now completely unclasp your hands and re-clasp them-but this time, put your opposite thumb on the top. How does it feel?

Now cross your arms in front of you. Notice which arm is on the top. Left or right? Next, completely uncross your arms and then recross them with the opposite arm on the top. Feel a little odd? What you have just experienced is what a physical habit feels like.

Are habits bad? Absolutely not! I have a habit of driving on the right side of the road and stopping at red lights. These are good habits. I get pretty upset when somebody gets "creative" with me on them.

Still, our habitual thinking tends to get in the way when we want to create new ideas. Many of us tend to run with the first idea we come up with, even if it causes us to run off the edge of a cliff.

How do you deal with a habit that's not productive for you, a habit that's not working for you? My psychologist friends say that the best way to deal with such a habit is to replace it with a habit that is working for you. So the next time you have a tough problem to solve, consider some creativity habits. Ask yourself:

∗"How else can I do this?"
∗"What if...?"
∗"How can I use something that doesn't fit with this at all?"

The philosopher Socrates has often been paraphrased, "When you always do what you've always done, you always get what you've always got." Now, if you like what you're getting, that's terrific. But if you want to make some changes in what's going on in your organization, that's good reason to begin using some new creativity habits. By the way, if the Socrates phrase doesn't work for you, try this one: "Insanity is doing the same thing over and over while expecting different results."

Two: Ask Questions

Voltaire once said, "Judge a person by his questions rather than his answers" It is important for leaders to ask questions— yet I admit it can be difficult. Aren't leaders supposed to have all the answers? They are the experts, after all. They have made it to the top by giving answers and directions. Unfortunately, in many organizations, as leaders rise closer to the top, they become more isolated and out of touch with the daily business. So asking questions is crucial.

There are two basic kinds of questions:

* *Legitimate questions* designed to get more information;
* *Bogus questions* designed to put subordinates on the defensive.

Make sure the questions you ask are open, then be ready to receive an answer. Questions that provoke defensive responses probably will not get you the information you need. Someone who thinks he is being blamed for something isn't likely to be especially helpful.

The most effective research scientists are not the ones with all the answers, but the ones who ask questions. They are forever curious about everything. Part of asking questions is being unafraid to appear stupid. Voltaire said of a know-it-all of his generation, "He must be very ignorant, for he answers every question he is asked."

Three: Use Passive Ways to Generate Ideas

Don't neglect the passive ways to get new ideas that come to you almost for "free." Face it, as leaders most of us don't get our best ideas at work. Participants in my seminars and classes usually report that they get their best ideas while driving a car, taking a bath or shower, or as they fall asleep at night.

While at work, most of us are in the implementation mode, the action mode, the make-it-happen mode. When we get away from work and are able to pay attention to something in a relaxed way, new ideas begin to surface. Activities like driving, bathing, or falling asleep are so automatic that we relax the judgmental part of our thinking, thus allowing new ideas to surface.

The key is to be ready to catch those ideas when they appear. Keep a piece of paper, a note pad, or a pocket tape recorder with you to record these new insights. A friend of mine calls his voice mail with his new ideas so he can listen to them when he gets back to his office. Use what ever method works for you to capture your insights.

Four: Vary Your Routine

It's no surprise that many of us get great ideas for work-related problems when we are on vacation. When you go on vacation, you significantly alter your routine. You aren't keeping your regular hours. You aren't in familiar surroundings. You aren't exposed to the situations that you face in a usual work day. One of my colleagues, Dr. Gerard Puccio, says there is a direct relationship between the distance he is away from home and the number of new ideas he generates. For Gerard, the farther away from home, the more ideas he creates.

Now, I'm not suggesting that every time you need a new concept you should leave town; but there are some definite ways to adapt this approach. Here are a couple:

A. Treat your commute time as a scenic vacation. Instead of thinking about what is going to happen at the office, focus on the world around you; take a mini-vacation on the way to work. Drive to work a different way, or get off the expressway and take the scenic route. By exposing yourself to some different scenery, you are likely to get some new input. Ride the train to work? Then sit on the opposite side you usually sit on and look out the window instead of burying your nose in the morning paper.

B. Vary your routine at home. Do you always go to the same place on Friday night for dinner? Do you always go to a movie on the week-end? Try a different approach. Instead of going to a movie, go to a hockey game. Stay home. Take a walk. Have a barbecue on a boat. Don't see many foreign films? Then go see a movie with subtitles.

John Gardner, in his book *On Leadership*, interviewed a number of leaders and noted that most of their solutions for renewal could be summed up in a brief line of advice: "Do something nonverbal."[1] Music, nature, sensory enjoyment, working with one's hands, gardening, or sports opened these leaders up to new possibilities. The same is true for you.

Five: Read and Listen to a Variety of Material

Several years ago, a study was done on the reading habits of scientists.[2] Researchers grouped the scientists into three categories. The first group was labeled "innovative"; these scientists exhibited the highest creative productivity as measured by patents. The second group was labeled "productive"; these scientists were known for being technically proficient. The third group was labeled "slugs"; they were neither innovative nor productive.

The study found that "slugs" read almost nothing. The "productive" scientists read almost exclusively in their field, while the "innovative" scientists (who were not always as technically up-to-date as their "productive" colleagues) read in a variety of fields. In fact, a great deal of the latter group's reading was outside of their area of expertise. These scientists read everything from science fiction to technical journals, from *Popular Mechanics* to *Psychology Today*, and therefore enjoyed a much richer storehouse of information from which to generate new concepts.

A friend of mine (a leader in a food service organization) tells the young college graduates who work with him that "If you want to find out what's going on in the food service industry today, read *Institutional Management* or *Restaurant News*. But if you want to find out what's going to be going on in this field in the future, read *Psychology Today*."

In other words, you can read all the technical stuff in your field to find out what's going on. But to spot the trends of the future and to get new information, you need to read outside of your area.

Don't have time to read? Then listen to tapes in your car. But don't listen to tapes that focus solely on your particular business; buy self-improvement tapes, books on tape, and mysteries. Most public libraries offer a variety of cassettes and compact disks. The old radio dramas were wonderful for exciting listeners' imaginations. Use the rich resource of recorded material whenever you drive.

Always listen to the same radio station with the same

music programming? Try an all-news station or National Public Radio. Use your drive time to keep your mind fresh and refreshed. And of course, keep that tape recorder nearby so when new ideas surface, you can effortlessly record them.

Six: Network

Beyond reading and listening to varied material, it's important to interact with people from varying backgrounds who have a variety of interests. This isn't always easy to do, for most of us find it more comfortable to spend time with people familiar to us. To our own detriment we don't make the time or effort to meet new people.

Research conducted on communication networks determined that the best source of new information is not from the people you see regularly.[3] Why not? They usually have the same information you do. The best source of new information is from other networks—people who run in circles different from your own (also known as non-homogeneous groups).

To stimulate your creativity, it is important to tap into groups of people with whom you usually don't interact. Find those new networks and plug into them.

Seven: Develop Personal Support Systems

It is crucial to have in place the personal and professional relationships that can provide you with a support system when the going gets tough. According to Dr. Perry Buffington, nationally known psychologist, lecturer, and media personality, the old saying "It's lonely at the top" is a huge understatement.[4] Buffington has worked with leaders in many corporations across the country who have climbed to the top of the corporate ladder. He has found that when these people finally reach the top, they look at their world and say, "Oh no—I'm alone!"

Soon it dawns on them that they're not just alone, they are *really* alone. They begin to realize, *I may be missing something—the cold, hard cash and the rise to power may have cost me more than I realized.* This realization indirectly turns them into more "human" people because they still have a need to be affiliated with others. As a result, they start to reach out. And, according to Buffington, when you start reaching out to others, you start trying to solve human problems. You begin to do creative problem solving.

The importance of a social support system was reported by Dr. Joan Borysenko in her book *Minding the Body, Mending the Mind* in this dramatic account:

> Several years ago, the small town of Roseto, Pennsylvania, raised considerable interest in the scientific community because of its very low rate of death from coronary heart disease. Epidemiologists began to study the Rosetans, expecting to find low levels of the major risk factors for coronary heart disease: cigarette smoking, fat consumption, a sedentary lifestyle, and obesity. They got a big surprise. The Rosetans had terrible health habits. They were high in all the risk factors.
>
> It turned out that their protective factor was actually the social fabric of the community. The extended family was alive and well. People tended to stay within Roseto, and so there was a great deal of closeness. People knew one another, their family histories, their joys and sorrows. In Roseto there were plenty of people to listen and to lend a hand when needed. Statistics revealed that when people moved out of Roseto, their rate of heart attacks rose to the predicted level. Social support, the great stress buffer, turned out to be more important than health habits in predicting heart disease.[5]

Conclusion: As a leader you need people to talk with, people with whom you can share your joys and challenges. Nurture those support systems, whether it is family or friends. It might save your life!

Eight: Stop the Action

The peace of solitude is difficult to attain in our culture. We are constantly bombarded with things to do, to buy, and to change. Yet all great leaders and teachers have taken time out of their busy schedule for meditation, rest, and reflection.

The gospels report that Jesus spent forty days in the wilderness undergoing temptation by the devil before returning to proclaim his message of salvation. It is said that Gandhi spent from midnight on Sunday night to midnight Monday night in solitude, fasting, prayer, and meditation.

When you remove yourself from your habitual, fast-paced environment, new self-understanding is possible. Anthony Storr in his book *Solitude: A Return to the Self*, recounted how Admiral Byrd manned an Antarctic advanced weather base in the winter of 1934. Byrd called it a form of renewal and said, "I wanted something more than just privacy in the geographical sense. I wanted to sink roots into some replenishing philosophy ... I wanted to be by myself for a while and to taste peace and quiet and solitude long enough to find out how good they really are."[6] Byrd summed up his long solitude like this: "I did take away something that I had not fully possessed before; appreciation of the sheer beauty and miracle of being alive, and a humble set of values . . . I live more simply now, and with more peace"

I take time out by sitting quietly in my enclosed porch, gazing out over my tree-lined back yard. Don't have the opportunity to sit quietly at home for more than thirty seconds? Then try the approach a friend of mine uses. He often leaves work early and stops at a park near his home. He will sit in his car, gazing quietly over the park for thirty minutes. He says this method works extraordinarily well for him. He gets some time to renew himself, to reflect, and he doesn't create an imposition on his family or business associates.

Any form of solitude will work. Spend thirty minutes sitting quietly in a comfortable chair. Don't read, listen to music, fall asleep, eat, or watch television. Just sit. In the first ten minutes your mind will race and will tell you all the things you should be doing. Resist the temptation to get up and act. This is your renewal time. After those first excruciating ten minutes, sitting will become easier. New insights might come forth. The important thing is to take a "time out" in your life. If you want some new ideas, make some space for them. By stopping the action, you create room for those new ideas to come in.

Nine: Create an Environment that Encourages Creativity
Have you ever walked into a place, rubbed your hands together, and said to yourself, "I could really do some great work here"?

Artists and musicians have studios, craftsmen have workshops, professors and pastors have studies, and scientists have laboratories. Sitting in a room with a view of the ocean or looking out the window of my office at the pine trees in my back yard does this for me.

Where is your creative space? Where do you go to do your best work?

My friend Tracey Jung, a professional artist, describes her studio as her sanctuary. It is her "safe place." When she is in her studio, she is able to create, try out new concepts, and leave her work in progress. Her studio is filled with light, it's clean and well organized and is just the right temperature for Tracey. It is also the place where no one disturbs her. It is her retreat from the hectic, outside world, a place where she can immerse herself in a private world of concepts and colors.

In his book, *The Art and Science of Creativity*, George Kneller described the unusual devices some creative people adopted for their working environments.[7] Schiller loved the smell of apples, so he filled his desk with rotten ones; Proust worked in a cork-lined room; Mozart composed after exercise; Frost would write only at night; Dr. Johnson surrounded himself with a purring cat, orange peel, and tea; Hart Crane played jazz loudly on a Victrola. The extreme case was the philosopher Kant, who would work in bed at certain times of the day with the blankets arranged around him in a specific fashion. While writing *The Critique of Pure Reason*, Kant would concentrate on a tower visible from his window. When some trees grew up to hide the tower, he became frustrated, and the city fathers of Konigsberg cut down the trees so that he could continue his work.

Now, I am not advocating that you stock your desk with decaying fruit or cut down the trees in your neighborhood. But think about it for a minute: What are the attributes of your optimal working environment?

Do you do your best work with music playing or in silence? Are you a morning person or an evening person? Is your space filled with light, or is it dim? Is it cool or warm? Do you sip coffee or snack while you work? Is your ideal work environment formal or informal? Do you have desks and tables neatly arranged in your space, or is your area informal with pillows and cushions scattered about the place?

Drs. Rita and Ken Dunn have developed a survey designed to diagnose the conditions under which individuals are most likely to learn, achieve, create, or solve problems.[8]

Their *Productivity Environmental Preference Survey* (PEPS) identifies factors that are important for a person's optimal working environment. These factors include: sound, light, temperature, formal or informal design, structure of task, intake required or not required, peak time of day, and others.

Many studies have supported the validity of the Dunns' conclusions. One such study, reported by Krimsky, tested students who preferred learning in a brightly lit environment and those who preferred the opposite set of conditions.[9] Reading speed and accuracy scores were consistently and significantly higher when the instructional lighting environment matched the students' diagnosed preference for style of light.

What is your preferred working environment? What kind of environment helps you become the most comfortable and productive? James Adams in his book *Conceptual Blockbusting* suggests designing the all-purpose studio.[10] This is the environment in which you can create, paint, write, invent, design, or craft.

Remember, if you expect yourself to do creative work–and you should if you want your company to succeed and thrive–then you need a place to do it. When you begin to more closely examine your working style preferences and change your environment to support your preferences, you will not only increase your creativity, but you will increase your productivity as well.

Ten: Create a Healthy Lifestyle

The brain requires neurohormones or neurotransmitters in order to function, and it can work only within the confines of the neurotransmitters it has available. Twenty years ago, scientists knew of only two neurotransmitters. We now know of sixty neurotransmitters and neurophysiologists estimate there may be as many as 300 in the brain.

What are these neurotransmitters made of? They are long chain polypeptides that are made of amino acids. Amino acids come from proteins and carbohydrates. Complex carbohydrates like whole grains, legumes, and whole vegetables are most useful for the overall health of our body. If we modify our diet to increase the intake of complex carbohydrates, we increase the biological availability of these amino acids to build neurotransmitters. When you increase the building blocks of neurotransmitters, which are complex carbohydrates, cognitive function increases.

Advice for leaders: *Cut down on the fat and increase complex carbohydrates.* You will think better.

Exercise is another crucial component of a healthy lifestyle. A regular, rhythmic training regime (once you have reached a basic state of fitness) is essential. According to Robert Eckert—Senior partner in the consulting firm "New and Improved"—regular exercise releases the neuropeptides norepinephrine, dopamine, and seratonin. These three neuropeptides significantly aid clearer thinking. Cocaine, caffeine and nicotine release and somewhat imitate these same three neuropeptides in the brain, but only for short periods. So, yes, after someone ingests cocaine, drinks coffee, or smokes a cigarette, they will enjoy a brief period of clearer thinking. Of course, there are many terrible side effects (enough said).

Exercise causes a person to think more clearly and, for some time after exercising, to be more motivated. As a result, expect a higher level of ideation after exercise and the motivation to stay on task longer. I have found this to be true in my own creative productivity. When I am working on a creative project and I exercise later in the day, I am able to think clearly and work efficiently well into the evening. Without that exercise break, I can become lethargic and the only productivity I get is channel surfing on cable television. I have a stationary bicycle to get my aerobic exercise and I also do some stretching and strength building exercises.

Advice to leaders: *Develop a regular exercise routine and stick to it.* You will think more clearly and be more productive.

Eleven: Reawaken Your Sense of Humor
Dr. Joel Goodman, Director of the HUMOR Project, Inc. in Saratoga Springs, New York, states that humor and creativity are intimately related (or at least "kissing cousins").[11] At gut level, when you find something funny, you laugh: "Ha-ha!"

When you make a creative breakthrough, it's not unusual to say, "Aha, I've got it!" or "Aha, why didn't I think of that before?" The creative breakthrough and a response to humor feel the same, and in some ways are the same. Humor and creativity bring together two different concepts that were originally considered unrelated. In creativity, those unrelated concepts produce a new idea; in humor, those unrelated concepts produce a joke. Therefore, one way to indirectly develop your creativity is to nurture your sense of humor.

Goodman provided the following five recommendations for developing your sense of humor, and in turn nurturing your own creativity.

A. Develop your comic vision. We are all living in the same world. Why is it that people like Jerry Seinfeld or Ellen DeGeneres or Bill Cosby can look at the same chunk of reality and see humor in it, where other mere mortals look at it and go, "Duh"? It's because they've developed their comic vision. One very simple tip for you to develop a comic vision: take five minutes a day to stop the action, call a mental time-out, step off the treadmill and just look for the humor around you. Make believe you're Allen Funt of the old television program *Candid Camera*. Once you begin to look for humor, humor finds you.

B. Model a sense of humor. If you want to encourage humor in other people, then have some fun yourself. Joel Goodman cites the extraordinary results that Southwest Airlines has produced under the leadership of Herb Kelleher. Kelleher has a tremendous sense of humor that permeates his entire organization. The Herb Kellehers of the world model humor in leadership and show that year after year, the bottom line and the funny line can go together. By the way, Southwest Airlines has been in the black for the last twenty five years, in an industry that has lost billions of dollars in recent years.

C. Be true to yourself. One of the misconceptions Dr. Goodman tries to puncture is that humor is merely joke-telling. When some leaders hear about humor in the workplace they think, *Oh, I'm supposed to be a stand-up comedian, which is neither appropriate nor professional. Besides, it's not my forte.*

But humor is far more than joke-telling. When you are using humor as a leader, be true to yourself. Utilize it according to your own personality and style and realize that humor, although it may include joke-telling, goes way beyond jokes to focus on those things and events in life that tickle your funny bone. If something tickles your funny bone, use it to tickle the funny bones of others.

D. Humor, like creativity, can be used for positive or negative ends. Humor can be used to create, build relationships, bring people together, and improve morale; or it can be used to put people down, destroy self-esteem, and undermine teamwork. How do you use humor? Do you use it as a tool to build people up and bring folks together, or as a weapon to tear people down and tear them apart? As Joel Goodman emphasizes, there is a difference between laughing *at* others and laughing *with* others. The more a leader can model laughing *with* others and minimize laughing *at* others, the healthier will be the environment for self-esteem, as well as for creativity.

E. Let people know that while you are serious about your goals, quotas, and mission, you don't take yourself too seriously. Joel distinguishes between serious and solemn leaders. We need to be serious professionals, but solemnity doesn't serve either in the short run or in the long run. Being able to laugh at yourself and tell a joke on yourself (where it's appropriate) helps you not only to halt destructive self-criticism, but helps others take it easier on themselves as well.

Twelve: Be Passionate About Your Positive, Compelling Future Vision

In 1953 a study was conducted on the Yale University graduating class.[12] Students were asked if they had written down plans to accomplish specific goals in their lives. Three percent had written their goals and had made plans to accomplish them. Twenty years later, in 1973, the surviving members of the class were interviewed. The results were astounding. The three percent who had written down their goals were worth more financially than the entire other 97 percent combined.

Why the difference? The three percent created something significant they needed to do in their future. Instead of allowing their future to be predicted by their past, they were "pulled" toward this future by a positive future image. They created something they were passionate about and compelled to do.

The eminent creativity researcher Dr. E. Paul Torrance, the inventor of the Torrance Tests of Creative Thinking and author of countless articles and books on creativity, stressed the importance of "falling in love with something." In his article, "The Importance of Falling in Love with 'Something,'" he emphasized the power of this positive future image:

> My experience and research have increasingly made me aware of the dreadful importance of falling in love with "something"–a dream, an image of the future. I am convinced that the driving force behind future accomplishments is the image of the future of people. Positive images of the future are a powerful and magnetic force. These images of the future draw us on and energize us, giving us courage and will to take important initiatives and move forward to new solutions and achievements. To dream and to plan, to be curious about the future and to wonder how much it can be influenced by our efforts are important aspects of our being human ... life's most energizing and exciting moments occur in those split seconds when our strugglings and searchings are suddenly transformed into the dazzling aura of the profoundly new, an image of the future.[13]

In the same article, Torrance reported, "scientists have accumulated considerable evidence that our image of the future is a powerful motivating force and determines what we are motivated to learn and achieve . . . a person's image of the future may be a better predictor of future attainment than his past performances."[14]

Torrance has conducted many studies on creative and gifted children. One such study was a twenty-two-year longitudinal study of elementary school children that began in 1958. As part of this study, Torrance asked these children to tell him what they were in love with. Some consistently said they didn't know, others were inconsistent, changing their future images each year. But about half of the children in this study were consistent in their choices and persisted in careers consistent with the future career images they expressed as children. Torrance reported that, "future career images proved to be a significant predictor of . . . creative adult achievement. As a matter of fact, this indicator (having or not having a future image that they were in love with) was a better predictor of adult creative achievement than indexes of scholastic promise and attainment in school."[15]

In fact, some of Torrance's students had images of their future as early as the second, third, and fourth grade. Recall your own elementary school days. What was it that you really wanted to do when you were a child? What were your dreams? What was it that you imagined would fill you with joy as you grew older? Are you living that dream now?

Your role as creative leader for your company is to set a vision for your organization and then stick to it. This vision should be based on the strengths of your company and where you want the company to go.

Barry Sudburry, vice president of research and development at the Clorox Company, told me that he sees his role as "pointing the arrow toward the future" and then allowing his people to get the company there. "My job is to remove the blocks and barriers that prevent my people from using their creativity to move toward that vision," he says.

You can do the same thing. Express your vision in the value you want to give to your customer, the kinds of products and services you want your company to be known for, and the ways your staff will work together. Work with your people to translate that vision into objectives that create specific and measurable results, then give them the tools they will need to accomplish those objectives. It is crucial to train your people in the skills that will help them get the job done and to think more creatively. Be ready and willing to coach and support when necessary. Then stay out of their way! Let them do the job; they will create the results.

MASKS–AND CREATIVITY–FIRST

My business requires a lot of flying in airplanes. At the beginning of every flight there's a safety demonstration detailing what should be done if the cabin loses pressure. I'm instructed to put on my oxygen mask first, and only then to help a child or someone else who needs my assistance.

In the same way that airlines instruct passengers to put on their own masks before helping others, so leaders must nurture their own creativity before they attempt to enhance the creativity of others in their organizations. How can an organization grow and survive and thrive if the oxygen or the life blood of the organization—creativity—is cut off?

So think of this chapter as my pre-flight instructions to you before we take to the skies of creativity. *Always* put on your own mask before you try helping others strap on their masks. That is, learn and practice many ways of keeping yourself growing in creativity. When you have done that—and only then—will you be ready to help others around you.

In the same way that an oxygen-deprived brain would be of no use to anyone on a plane in trouble, so is a creativity-starved leader of little use to an organization that has run into some serious turbulence.

So get your mask on. Nurture your own creativity. And come fly the fruitful skies!

Phrase Problems in a Way They Can Be Solved

A problem properly stated is half solved.
JOHN DEWEY

Albert Einstein once was asked, "If some imminent disaster threatened the world and you had one hour in which you knew you could save it, how would you spend your time?"

Einstein thought a moment and then replied, "I would spend the first fifty-five minutes identifying the problem and the last five minutes solving it. For the formulation of a problem is often far more essential than its solution, which may be merely a matter of mathematical or experimental skill."[1]

Einstein's answer is right on target, not only for saving the world, but also for saving your business. If you want your company to succeed in the marketplace, it's crucial to view problems and talk about them in a way they can be solved.

IS CREATIVITY JUST GENERATING IDEAS?

Think about the last time you tackled a tough problem in your business or personal life. How did you spend your time? Did you immediately race off to take action on what you thought was a solution to your problem—only to discover later that what you thought was the problem really wasn't and that the action you took was ineffective?

A major misconception about creativity is that it consists entirely in generating ideas for solving problems. Should you review the creativity books on the market today, you would see that most volumes focus solely on generating ideas.

But generating ideas is only part of the creative process. A great deal of creativity is needed to discover the real problem. That is why, instead of rushing off to explain a variety of techniques to generate "breakthrough" ideas, we will now focus on defining the problem. One way to be more effective in business is to consciously work to understand your problem *before* you generate ideas or take action to solve it.

And make no mistake—properly defining the problem can save you thousands, even millions, of dollars. Consider the following true account taken from the book *Thinkertoys* by Michael Michalko.

In the 1950s, experts believed the ocean-going freighter was dying. Costs were rising, and it took longer and longer to get merchandise delivered. This increased pilferage at the docks as goods piled up waiting to be loaded.

The shipping industry formulated its challenge as: "In what ways might we make ships more economical at sea and while in transit from one port to another?"

They built ships that were faster or required less fuel, and reduced crew size. Costs still kept going up, but the industry kept concentrating its efforts on reducing the specific costs related to ships while at sea and doing work.

They were doing things right, but they weren't doing the right thing. They were about as effective as an expert salesperson who spends all her energy, time, and talents trying to sell veal door-to-door.

A ship is capital equipment and the biggest cost for capital equipment is the cost of *not working*, because interest has to be paid without income being generated to pay it. Finally, a consultant stretched the industry's challenge to: "In what ways might the shipping industry reduce costs?"

This allowed the industry to consider *all* aspects of shipping, including loading and stowing. The innovation that saved an industry was to separate loading from stowing, by doing the loading on land, before the ship reaches port. It is much quicker to put on and take off preloaded freight. They decided to concentrate on the costs of *not working* rather than *working*, and reduce the amount of time a freighter does not work. The answer was the roll-on, roll-off ship and the container ship.

This simple solution was the direct result of reframing the challenge. The outcome has been startling. Freighter traffic has increased fivefold in the last thirty years, and costs are down by 60 percent. Port time has been reduced by three quarters, and with it, congestion and theft.[2]

Note that the shipping industry didn't escape extinction by generating boatloads of creative ideas to solve its problems; the breakthrough came by redefining the problem from "In what ways might we make ships more economical at sea and while in transit from one port to another?" to "In what ways might the shipping industry reduce costs?" Amazingly, the modern shipping industry owes its continued existence to a consultant who knew how to ask the right question. He didn't ask, "How can we generate hundreds of ideas," but "Which problem is the right one to solve?"

OUR LANGUAGE DICTATES HOW WE VIEW A PROBLEM

The consultant in the previous story understood that the language we use to describe a problem is crucial. Most of us don't know how to accurately describe the problem or challenge that confronts us. So it is not surprising that we have trouble solving problems. It is also not surprising that we sometimes feel overwhelmed when our problems appear too great or we can't decide where to start.

Consider the challenges facing the steel industry in recent times. The integrated steel process has been uneconomical since it was invented in the 1870s. It begins with iron ore, creating very high temperatures four times only to quench them, then transports masses of metal over great distances. The only time the industry performed well was in times of war. You might say it was a lump in America's gravy.

Since the early 1970s, the demand for steel had been going up. To meet the demand, however, integrated steel mills had to add new units, which required a substantial investment. Since demand rises in small steps, the expansion would not be profitable until the demand reached the mill's new capacity. If a mill chose not to expand, it would lose its customers. In the steel business, if you can't deliver orders on time, customers don't wait; they go elsewhere. Faced with this choice, companies expanded. Consequently, firms were profitable only for that time when demand reached the new capacity. When the demand exceeded that capacity, the integrated mills would be forced to expand again.

Finally a group of new, young managers stepped in and asked aggressive questions about every step of the integrated steel-making process. The young questioners asked, "Why? Why do mills have to get larger to meet demand?" Simply by asking "Why?" they discovered that the steel industry violated the basic laws of economics. By shifting their perspective from increasing mill size to increasing throughput, they proposed a shift from the giant, ever-expanding integrated plant to a mini-mill.

A mini-mill can be built for one-tenth the cost of an integrated plant, uses heat only once and does not quench it, starts with steel scrap instead of ore, and ends up with one final product (for example, beams, rods, etc.). The mini-mills offer modem technology, low labor costs, and target markets.

One executive boldly declared that if these young men had not asked the right questions, we would still be making steel the old-fashioned way—and companies would still be having a hard time making a consistent profit.

Examples like this show how crucial it is to describe the problem in a way that your mind considers solvable. If you believe the difficulty is insurmountable, you won't spend any time trying to discover a way to overcome it. And therefore the problem won't get solved.

CHALLENGE THE PROBLEM
Perhaps the first step toward correctly defining a problem is to recognize that problems sometimes come in disguise. That is, what we think is the problem might not be the real problem at all.

Take the shipping industry story, for example. One of the things that prevented the shipping experts from solving the problem was that they were looking at the problem too narrowly. "In what ways might the shipping industry reduce cost?" is a much broader view of the problem than, "In what ways might we make ships more economical at sea and while in transit from one port to another?" The first problem statement tells your mind to generate much broader, more far-reaching ideas. The latter problem statement provides a very narrow range of possible ideas. "In what ways might the shipping industry reduce costs?" allows you to generate more options from a much broader perspective.

In another example, "How might I live a richer, more satisfying life?" is a much broader problem statement than "How might I raise the money to buy a new house?" Problems vary in their levels of abstraction or concreteness. For example, "How might I live a more healthy lifestyle?" is much more abstract than "How might I find time to exercise?"

SQUEEZE THE CHALLENGE FURTHER

You can almost always squeeze more out of a challenge. Once you have asked the key questions, go one step further—ask "How else?" and "What else?" That's how one company not only distinguished itself from its competitors, but forged to the head of the pack.

You've probably heard of O.M. Scott & Co. It's a leader in lawn-care products, specializing in seeds, fertilizer, pesticides, and related items. Only a few years ago the company didn't amount to much more than a fly buzzing about the heads of corporate giants such as Sears Roebuck and Co. and Dow Chemical. While people liked Scott's products, they didn't consider them any better than those of their competitors.

The challenge for Scott was to improve its market share. But how to do this? After generating several problem statements, eventually the company settled on one: "In what ways might we differentiate our products from the others?"

This was tougher than it may appear. Why? Because in general, all lawncare products are similar. At that time every company insisted its products were "scientific" and gave long, detailed instructions to users on how the product should be applied, given certain soil conditions and temperatures. The result? Customers came away convinced that proper lawn care is difficult and depends on precise, inflexible practices dictated by science. continued on page 48

continued from page 47

When Scott's sales force asked the public how the company might grab a competitive advantage in the market-place, what kept coming up was customer frustration with lawncare methods. So Scott brain-stormed ways to alleviate the frustration. As a result, the company's problem statement changed to, "In what ways might we alleviate customer frustrations with planting?"

By asking "How else?" and "What else?" Scott developed ideas ranging from more friendly directions to gardening classes for customers. Then came the idea that made millions: a simple, mechanical contraption called the Scott Spreader. This small, lightweight wheel-barrow features holes at the bottom that can be set to allow the proper quantities of Scott's products to pass through in an even flow. Before the Scott Spreader, no lawncare supplier had given its customers a tool to *control* the process. Scott designed its product line around the Spreader, and overnight this small seed retailer became the market leader in lawncare.

That's what can happen when you squeeze a challenge just a bit further.

When we challenge the problem, we are enabled to look at the problem in a number of ways and view the situation from a number of perspectives.

In each of the two examples, for instance, the first problem statements are much broader in scope than the second ones. Let's generate a few ideas for both of them.

Ideas that could be generated for living a richer, more satisfying life might include:

* Increasing your income
* Having more meaningful relationships with your family
* Leading your company more effectively
* Developing an investment strategy for retirement
* Raising the money to buy a new house

DON'T PLAY FLAVOR OF THE MONTH

Any sort of organizational change which includes an emphasis on creativity requires your people to acquire a new skill. It is difficult for people to change and begin operating in a different way. Existing support systems are geared to the old organization, so when something new is introduced, some members of the organization are bound to hold back. They don't get involved. Unfortunately, after a year or eighteen months, management often looks at the program and says, "Look-we're getting only minimal outcomes, so let's go on to something else. Let's change to another program."

In fact, by failing to follow through and by changing from one program to another, the work force is being trained *not* to get involved and *not* to participate. When the next program is introduced, previously involved workers will hold back because of the disruption caused when the last program failed. In this way employees are trained to withhold their involvement from new initiatives.

Once a commitment is made to infuse creativity skills into an organization, it is crucial that management commit to the method and enforce and reinforce its use. It must not play "flavor of the month" when the chosen program does not produce results in the short term. Remember, infusing creativity into an organization is a long-term commitment. You won't reap its tremendous benefits if you don't give it a real chance to work.

Ideas that could be generated for living a more healthy lifestyle might include:

- ✶ Improving your diet
- ✶ Getting more rest
- ✶ Quitting smoking
- ✶ Finding an exercise routine that works for you
- ✶ Scheduling more time to exercise

The problem statements, "How might I live a richer, more satisfying life?" and "How might I live a more healthy lifestyle?" are broader and more inclusive than "How might I raise the money to buy a house?" or "How might I schedule time to exercise?"

When we try to tackle problems which have been defined either too broadly or too narrowly, we often run into trouble. Allow me to give an example.

I have sometimes worked with sales groups on the problem statement, "How might we increase sales?" This, of course, is a very broad problem statement. There are thousands of ways to increase sales, from more advertising to better customer service to better account retention. If we were to focus this problem more narrowly, we might ask, "How might we increase the number of prospects we generate through telephone marketing?" This query more sharply focuses our ability to generate problem statements than does the broad question, "How might we increase sales?"

On the other hand, narrowly focused questions are not always the most helpful. The best problem statements are not necessarily the most narrowly focused. For example, the problem statement, "How might I buy a car?" is very narrow; only a few ideas might be generated from a problem statement like this. Some ideas that come to mind:

∗Go to a car dealership
∗Look in the newspaper for used cars
∗Talk to your friends to see if they know someone who is selling a car
∗Buy a used car

Of course, a problem statement like this assumes you already have the necessary money or credit to buy a car. What if you don't? "How might I raise the money for buying a car?" might be a second problem statement. Usually, however, for a problem like buying a car, applying a technique such as Creative Problem Solving is unnecessary. Most of us know how to buy a car–so just do it!

KEEPING THE COMPUTER SYSTEM UP AND RUNNING
Before we turn to some specific tools on how to phrase a problem correctly–that is, in a way that it can be solved–I'd like to describe how one company discovered that such correct phrasing provided the key to unlocking an enormous challenge.

How do you get a large organization of 400 people to buy into computer software systems changes, while at the same time keeping the system up, running, and available to dispatch service calls, distribute equipment and fulfill orders? That was the mega-challenge confronting Peter Pellegrino, Advanced Business Analyst and Team Leader for Change Management, when the Xerox corporation of Rochester, New York out-sourced the computers and software that supported its internal business process to EDS.

Peter said his company's massive undertaking presented innumerable problems. First, "there wasn't any process in place to make sure that we were planning for all the integration and the contingencies that were necessary," he said. "We also weren't doing any planning for testing the system."

Using Creative Problem Solving, Peter and his team immediately set to work. About six months later, they had devised a solution to their problem. Eventually more and more people were involved in the process, thus expanding the reach and effectiveness of the proposed solution. According to Peter,

> We spent a lot of time working with people to generate problem statements. We tried to tackle one problem statement at a time and take it through the process. We did an awful lot of brainstorming. From the very beginning, we wanted to make sure that we were getting buy-in from the entire organization. We didn't want to come up with this process in a vacuum and try to force it on an organization of 400 people. Creative Problem Solving was a powerful tool to help us re-engineer the organization.
>
> What ultimately made this project so successful was that everyone provided input on the problem statements and had the opportunity to participate in generating ideas. That really "salted it home" for a lot of people; they actually saw the ideas they were generating being put into practice.[3]

A variety of problem statements were generated in multitudes of problem identification sessions, including:
✶ "How might we make our established process work

using PCs in the client server enviroment?"
* "How might we make sure that it matches EDS's goals?"
* "How might we make sure it adds value to other EDS businesses outside of Xerox?"

After generating multiple problem statements, the group did more brainstorming to develop solutions to those problem statements. "This also helped us with our buy-in," Peter said, "because we had a whole new set of management that needed to be convinced that this process was the right thing to do, the right way to go, and that there was value added to it. We were very successful with that effort and right now our process is being expanded within the entire Xerox account.[4]"

So what was the bottom line of these efforts? I'll let Peter describe the final results:

> I can't think of an instance in the last two years in which we've implemented a new software change and caused the business to be unavailable due to the implementation. That's quite a track record for us.[5]

The key to EDS's success was not in generating multitudes of ideas, but in first relentlessly searching for problems. Peter's team looked for problems first, not for answers right away. Second, when they found a problem, they phrased the problem in a way it could be solved. Only then did they begin to generate ideas for solving the problem. Once that had been accomplished, success—and profitability—was the sweet result.

Leader, you simply can't go far wrong by following Albert Einstein's advice. If you want to succeed, spend some time making sure you're trying to solve the right problem. You can't save the world (or even your business) by generating a zillion ideas focused on the wrong problem. Remember Einstein's sage advice: "The formulation of a problem is often far more essential than its solution, which may be merely a matter of mathematical or experimental skill."

I may not understand the theory of General Relativity, but I can understand this statement. And I believe it!

So should you, if you want to lead a thriving business.

Don't Solve the Wrong Problem

Detecting the problem is as important as finding the answer.
E. R. HILGARD

How can we define problems effectively? How can we change our approach so that we discover the real problem? How can we avoid solving the wrong problem?

Remember the shipping industry example from the previous chapter? No one bothered to question what the real problem was. Everyone assumed the task was to create faster and more efficient ships, not to reduce time spent in port. Therefore, the real problem wasn't solved until someone asked the right question. Only then did the shipping industry find a way not only to survive, but thrive.

It cannot be said too strongly or too often: How we view a problem determines how we will solve it. Beware of the complicated solution to a problem! It could indicate that you are solving the wrong problem.

Let's now turn our attention to several tools that can help us become more effective in redefining a problem. All of these techniques will dramatically increase your ability to solve problems and move when opportunities arise.

THREE HELPFUL PHRASES
To help view a challenge as a problem that can be solved, I have found it helpful to use phrases such as: "How might we … ?""How to . . . ?"or "In what ways might we . . . ?"

For example, instead of describing your problem as: "We don't have any money to develop this project,"try phrasing the problem, "How might we reduce the cost of this project?"or "How might we raise the money?"Instead of saying: "Management will never buy this idea,"try, "How might we convince management of the value of this project?"or "How might we get management's support?"

PUT YOURSELF IN ANOTHER'S SHOES

For a long time bankers assumed that their customers preferred human tellers. Yet in the early 1980s, Citibank concluded that installing automatic tellers would help cut costs. Executives couldn't imagine that customers would actually prefer to deal with machines, however, so they reserved human tellers for people with more than $5,000 in their accounts. More modest depositors were relegated to the machines. It soon became clear that the machines were wildly unpopular, so Citibank stopped using them in 1983. Bank executives thought these events confirmed their belief that people simply disliked dealing with machines.

Some time later, another banker challenged this assumption. When he looked at the situation from a customer's perspective, he realized that the machines went unused because small depositors resented being treated as second-class customers. This banker restored the automatic tellers–this time, with no "class distinctions"–and they were an instant hit. Today, even Citibank reports that 70 percent of its transactions are handled by machine.

This banker challenged the dominant assumption by looking at it from the customer's perspective. A good way to challenge *any* assumption is by looking at it from someone else's perspective. Try writing a paragraph about your challenge as you see it. Next, change your perspective. If you're male, write it from a female standpoint; if you are a salesperson, write it from a customer's perspective; if you are a subordinate, write it from a superior's point of view. You might be surprised at how different the view looks from your adopted address.

The last two phrases in each example describe a problem that can be solved, while the first statements block your thinking. The first statements do nothing to provoke your imagination, nor do they give your mind any clue there might be a possible solution. Rather than suggest possibilities, they merely complain.

Using the phrases, "How might we . . . ?" "How to . . . ?" or "In what ways might we . . . ?"cues your mind that the problem confronting you just might be solvable. These phrases also "loosen up"the situation and encourage you to question what you originally thought was the only way to interpret the problem.

WITHHOLD JUDGMENT

The next time a tough problem confronts you, take out a legal pad and write your first impression of the problem. Then use the phrases "How to. . . ?" "How might I ... ?"or "In what ways might I . . . ?"to generate additional problem statements. Don't judge any of the problem statements you develop. Challenge yourself to write down at least thirty ways to restate the problem.

At first you will probably find this activity uncomfortable. Why? Because most of our training has taught us that as soon as we think we have identified the problem, we need to develop one right answer to solve it. The purpose of generating many problem statements is to develop a more effective definition of the problem, not to solve your problem right away. However, once you have the definition of the problem that provides you with a new insight, a new angle, or a different approach to deal with the problem, then generate ideas—but not before.

Great dividends will be yours when you spend time consciously challenging your first impression of the problem. In fact, this is the only way you're likely to discover, then solve, the real problem.

THE "WHY-WHY ELSE?" TECHNIQUE

One of the best ways to challenge your problem and to generate many possible problem statements is to use the delightful term, "Why?"Once you have developed a problem statement, ask "Why?"of that statement. After answering your own question, continue to ask, "Why else?"It's amazing what this simple technique can produce.

Like the other techniques sketched out in this book, the "Why-Why Else?"method can be used either in group or individual settings. For example, let's imagine that you are a minister and you are talking with a friend who is always asking questions. Sometimes she asks so many questions that you want to strangle her, but often her questions help you to look at your problem in a new way and focus on your real problem. One of the questions your friend constantly asks you is "Why?"

Let's drop in on a conversation between you and your friend on the problem of increasing attendance at your Sunday services.

"In what ways might I increase attendance at our Sunday morning worship services?"you ask.

"Why do you want to increase attendance at your Sunday morning worship services?"she replies.

"To build the church community."

"So your problem might be, `How might we build the church community?' I'm curious-why else do you want to increase attendance at Sunday morning worship services?"

"Because increased attendance energizes our Sunday morning services."

"So your problem might be, `In what ways might we energize our Sunday morning services?'"

"Hmm, I hadn't thought of that"

"Why else do you want to increase attendance at Sunday morning worship services?"

"Well, it's much better to look at people's faces than at the empty, shiny pew backs, and more people draws out the leadership in the church."

"All right, so your problem might be, `In what ways might we draw out the leadership in the church?'"

"That's an interesting way to look at this."

"So, tell me more. Why else do you want to increase attendance at Sunday morning worship services?"

"Because increased attendance stimulates our people to get involved in church ministry and mission life."

"So, your problem might be, `How might we stimulate our people to get involved in church ministry and mission life?'"

"Well, you have a point there."

"I know I might be pushing you here, but why else do you want to increase attendance at Sunday morning worship services?"

"Well, you know the church council has approved our plans to build a new church. More people increases the Sunday offering so we can add that money to the building fund."

"I see, so your problem might be, `How might we get more people to contribute to the building fund?'"

"That's another interesting point."

Are you ready to strangle your friend yet? Let's take a look at the different problem statements that your friend helped you to create. Your original problem statement was, "In what ways might I increase attendance at our Sunday morning worship services?" By asking "Why?" and "Why else?" your friend helped you create five more problem statements:

* How might we build the church community?
* In what ways might we energize our Sunday morning services?
* In what ways might we draw out the leadership of the church?
* How might we stimulate our people to get involved in church ministry and mission life?
* How might we get more people to contribute to the building fund?

LOWER THAT TRUCK

A classic story of solving the "wrong" problem occurred several years ago when a semi-tractor trailer truck got stuck as it tried to pass under a low clearance train trestle. The truck made it about halfway under the trestle before the top of the trailer wedged itself tightly into place. The truck could not move forward or backward; it was stuck.

Engineers and construction workers were brought in with cranes and other heavy equipment to dismantle part of the trestle, which would free the truck. A small crowd gathered to watch the activity. In the crowd was a boy of about eleven years of age. Suddenly he noticed something and

continued on page 58

continued from page 57

pushed himself through the crowd to the foreman who was directing the dismantling of the trestle.

"Hey mister, I think I know how to get the truck out of there."

"Yeah, sure kid," the foreman replied. "I don't have time to talk now. Can't you see I'm busy?"

The young boy persisted.

"But mister, I really do know how to get the truck out"

Finally, desperate to be left alone, the foreman turned to the youngster. "Okay, smart guy. How would you do this job?"

"The truck is too high to fit under the trestle, right?"

"Yes," the foreman replied gruffly.

"Instead of trying to raise the trestle, why don't you try lowering the truck?"

"What do you mean?" the foreman asked.

"Why don't you let some air out of the tires? Then he can probably back it out"

Of course, you know how the story ends. A sufficient amount of air was released from the truck tires, which lowered the truck enough so that it could easily be backed out from under the trestle.

The breakthrough for this problem didn't occur by generating more ideas to solve the problem as it was initially understood, but by redefining the problem from "How might we move the bridge?" to "How might we *remove* the truck?"

Any of the problem statements your friend helped you create could have been used as springboards for generating new ideas and could provide a new approach for solving the problem. For example, some of the ideas that could be generated to address those new problem statements are as follows:

* To build the church community you could plan community building activities like retreats or potluck dinners.
* To energize Sunday morning services you could include more music, interpretive dance, theater or even debates.

∗ To draw out the leadership in the church you could do leadership training or get members of the congregation involved in helping to deliver the Sunday morning service.

∗ To stimulate people to get involved in church min istry and mission life you could show films, videos, and statistics on the church's efforts in ministry and missions. You could invite missionaries to tell their stories.

∗ To get people to contribute to the building fund you could plan a fund drive, have key members of the church make public pledges and contributions, or even hold a "church building raising"telethon.

SELECT THE RIGHT PROBLEM STATEMENT

After you have created a number of ways to view your problem, you need to select the problem statement that goes to the root of the problem or that expresses the essence of what you would like to see happen. You need to select the problem statement that will provide a clear focus for the ideas you want to generate.

If you have been doing a good job of generating problem statements, you probably have at least thirty or forty of them. Now, how do you pick the problem statement(s) that is (are) really on target? It is a mistake merely to look over the list and pick one, unless you find a problem statement that is so captivating that it jumps off the page at you. Most of the time we aren't fortunate enough to have such a breakthrough in generating problem statements. Usually we need to deliberately look through the list and systematically select a problem statement that captures the ideal goal for which we want to generate ideas.

An excellent procedure for converging on key problem statements is called *highlighting*. Highlighting consists of four phases: *hits, relate to form hot spots, paraphrase,* and *select problem statement(s)*.

A. Hits

First, look through your list of problem statements. Do some of them look interesting to you or seem intriguing? Go

continued on page 60

continued from page 59

through your list and mark each one that does so. These are your "hits."Look for the problem statements that provide a new approach to the situation. Oftentimes these interesting and intriguing problem statements will stand head and shoulders above the rest; they'll almost jump off the page at you. Don't worry if you don't have an immediate way to solve that problem; that's what we will do next when we generate ideas.

If you are using the Brainstorming with Post-its technique (explained in chapter 6), mark the hits with a colored adhesive dot or with a marker. If you have listed your problem statements on paper, put a check mark or a star beside the hits. If you are writing your problem statements on paper, be sure you have numbered each of the problem statements so you can group together the problem statements that might relate to each other.

B. Relate or Cluster to Form Hot Spots

As you marked the hits, did you find that some seemed related—that naturally grouped together? In the next phase of highlighting, try to find those relationships. Look through the problem statements you have marked as hits. The hits that relate to each other form a "hot spot"A hot spot means that something is going on in this problem area which needs to be examined. If you are using Brainstorming with Post-its, move the Post-its that relate to each other into a cluster. If you have listed problem statements on paper, list the number of the hits that relate to each other on a separate sheet of paper.

C. Paraphrase or Restate

Now look over the hot spots. What does each one mean to you? What does each hot spot represent? Label it like a book title, but make sure that you phrase it in the form of a problem statement beginning with the words, "How to ... ?""How might I. . . ?"or "In what ways might I ... ?"This will help you to condense your thirty problem statements into probably five or six.

Resist the desire to string problem statements together into a long phrase. Problem statements should be concise

continued on page 61

continued from page 60
headlines of the problem you want to solve. Problem statements should be phrased as such and should clearly indicate who "owns"the problem. Problem statements should also indicate a clear action and a goal.

D. Select Your Problem Statement(s)

Now look over the hot spots you have labeled. Carefully determine if there is a hot spot that stands "head and shoulders"above the others. Which hot spot is outstanding? Make sure the hot spot is phrased in the form of a problem statement. Check to make sure that this is a problem for which you want to get some ideas. Often you will have several problem statements that are important to you, so pick the problem statement with which you want to begin. Once you have generated ideas to solve that problem, then work on the others.

Converging in this way provides a much more deliberate approach to selecting problem statements for which to effectively generate ideas. The result? You accomplish your overall goal, wish, challenge, or objective, one piece at a time.

If you generated ideas for all these problem statements, no doubt you would increase attendance at Sunday morning services, in addition to accomplishing several other objectives. But it's clear, for example, that drawing out church leadership is a very different problem statement than getting more people to attend church on Sunday morning.

THE "WHAT'S STOPPING ME?"TECHNIQUE

The "Why-Why else?"technique helps you to create a broader or more abstract definition of your problem. But sometimes the broader problem might not be the real problem (or at least it may not be the key that unlocks the real focus of the challenge). That's when the "What's stopping me?"technique can be very helpful.

The "What's stopping me?"technique will help you to approach the problem or see your challenge from a different perspective. It helps you avoid tunnel vision when you deal with your problem, and it gives you a systematic method or structure to consciously challenge the problem as you initially perceived it. Remember, many times what we think is our problem is not the real problem at all; half of creative problem solving is creative opportunity finding.

My students have often told me that the "What's stopping me?"technique challenges them to be extremely honest with themselves. Often, by asking "What's stopping me?"you discover that the key thing stopping you is *you,* or at least your fear of dealing with the problem.

To see how this technique works, let's revisit your questioning friend. But this time, instead of asking "Why"or "Why else,"she is asking, "What's stopping you?"and "What else is stopping you?"

"In what ways might I increase attendance at our Sunday morning worship services?"you ask.

"Tell me, what's stopping you from increasing attendance at Sunday morning worship services?"she replies.

"You know, sometimes I don't think our church members believe that it is an important part of our faith to invite others to worship."

"So, your problem might be, `How might we show our members the value of inviting other people to church?'"

"That's an interesting point."

"Tell me, what else is stopping you from increasing attendance at Sunday morning worship services?"

"Well, I think that many people have the idea that church is a drag. It is a boring, unenthusiastic time."

"So another way to look at your problem might be, `How might we show people how fun and interesting our church services can be?'"

"Hmm ... that's intriguing."

"I'm curious. What else is stopping you from increasing attendance at Sunday morning worship services?"

"Well, people have lots of demands on their time, and I'm not sure if Sunday morning is the best time for everyone. You know, I was thinking the other day about offering more times or opportunities for attendance. Something like longer store hours."

"That's an interesting point. So your problem might be, `How might we offer more times or opportunities for people to attend church?'"

"Yes, I think you have got something there."

"Tell me more. What else is stopping you from increasing attendance at Sunday morning worship services?"

"You know, the people who aren't there at our services don't know just how well we are doing. They don't know the 'product.' Frankly, I don't think we are advertising very well."

"Very interesting. So another way to look at your problem might be, `How might we advertise more effectively?' Let me ask you another question. What else is stopping you from increasing attendance at Sunday morning worship services?"

"Well, sometimes I think we aren't getting people to come back to church after they have been to a service or two."

"Okay, so your problem might be, `How might we get people to come back to church after their first or second visit?'"

"You know, you're absolutely right. Thanks! You have really helped me look at this problem in a new way."

Do you see how the "What's stopping me?"technique helps you become more concrete in the way you view your problem? Let's take a look at the kind of problem statements this method helped you create for solving your problem of increasing attendance at your Sunday morning worship services.

* How might we show our members the value of inviting other people to church?
* How might we show people how fun and interesting our church services can be?
* How might we offer more times or opportunities for people to attend church?
* How might we advertise more effectively?
* How might we get people to come back to church after their first or second visit?

Once again, these problem statements provide a markedly different angle to your problem of increasing attendance at Sunday morning worship services. If you were to generate ideas for solving any of these problems, chances are good that you would go a long way toward solving the problem you identified initially, but you might have other more powerful insights as well.

THE ROAD TO SUCCESS

If you want to be successful, it's crucial to phrase problems in a way they can be solved. Yet, in my experience, challenging our initial definition of a problem and developing a variety of ways to approach it is no easy task. It flies in the face of the way we've been taught to deal with problems.

From the time we were little tykes, we were taught that immediately upon recognizing something as a problem (or something that even smells like a problem), we should jump to ideas for solving it. Of course, that makes sense in an educational setting; most of those problems already have been well-defined. What is two plus two? Answer: Four.

But out in the world we find a different environment altogether. There we're constantly confronted with problems that lack definition. That's why it's crucial intentionally to try to redefine the real problem.

Second, we must also remember that the words we use to redefine problems dictate how we think about them. There's a very big difference between "We don't have the money to develop this project" and "How might we find the money to develop this project?" or "How might we reduce the cost?" The latter two tell your brain that this problem can be solved; the first provides only an obstacle. Language dictates how we view a problem and prompts the kinds of ideas we will use to solve that problem.

USING "WHY?" AND "WHAT'S STOPPING ME?"

Follow these six steps to use the "Why-Why else?" technique to change your view of a problem:

1. Phrase the challenge in the form of a problem statement, beginning with the words, "In what ways might I . . . ?" "How might I ... ?" or "How to . . . ?"
2. Ask "Why" and then answer the question.
3. Rephrase your answer in the form of another problem statement.
4. Ask "Why else" of the original problem statement, then answer it.
5. Turn your answer into another problem statement.

continued on page 65

continued from page 64

6. Continue asking "Why else"to help you find a new insight into your problem.

Follow these five steps to use the "What's stopping me?"technique:

1. Make sure your challenge is in the form of a problem statement.
2. Ask "What's stopping me?"and answer the question.
3. Rephrase your answer in the form of another problem statement.
4. As in the "Why else"process, ask "What else is stopping me?"of the original problem statement.
5. Continue to ask "What's stopping me?"of the original problem statement until the process confronts you with a new insight.

Problem statements can be broad or narrow in focus. They tell us the kinds of ideas we're going to generate. The broader the focus of the problem statement, the more wide ranging (and consequently unfocused) the ideas might be. The more narrow the focus of the problem statement, the more specific and readily actionable they might be. There probably isn't one correct definition of the problem, although some definitions are more likely to lead to success than others (given the particular circumstances). Some situations require a very well-defined problem statement; others call for much broader problem statements.

The key to determining the best problem statement is to challenge your initial definition of the problem by asking "Why?"or by asking "What's stopping me?"These will help you to find the appropriate statement of the problem. Then you can generate the ideas that will most effectively solve it.

Last, don't be afraid to go looking for problems; just know how to deal with them when you find them. Remember, the sooner you confront the problem and deal with it, the less stress you'll have.

Consider the advice of the character played by David Carradine in the 1970s television program, "Kung Fu."Kane would say this about his feelings: "I will know my fear. I will live my fear. I will experience my fear—and when it is gone, only I will remain."

Okay, so that sounds like something only a grasshopper might say. But it hints at a real truth. You can legitimately tell yourself, "I will seek out my problems. I will phrase the problems effectively. I will generate ideas to solve the problems— and then only the solutions will remain."

If you live by that motto, you'll avoid a problem not even the grasshopper himself could avoid. That is, the only thing that will get canceled is the problem that's keeping you from success.

FIVE

Defer Judgment and Generate Many Ideas

The best way to have a good idea is to have lots of ideas.
LINUS PAULING,
Nobel prize winner for chemistry and peace

"Yes, No! Right, Wrong! Too expensive, too cheap! Too slow, too fast! Too fast, too slow! It'll never fly, Orville"

Look out—you've just witnessed a judgment attack!

Every day in boardrooms and office meeting rooms across the United States, such negative judgments are thrown in the teeth of creative men and women looking for a better way to do business. And very often, these pessimistic words silence and kill the very ideas that could revolutionize an industry. Can you imagine how different our world might be had Orville Wright heeded such grim verbiage? Can you say "wagon train"?

But more to the point: How often do *you* use these words in your own business vocabulary?

Judgment, used at the wrong time, is one of the greatest inhibitors of creativity. If you want to become more creative, you must learn to consciously separate your imaginative thinking from your judgmental thinking. Only in that way will you be able to generate enough ideas to find the breakthroughs you seek.

OSBORN'S GUIDELINES
Alex Osborn-senior partner in the advertising agency Batten, Barton, Durstine, and Osborn (BBD&O), founder of the

Creative Education Foundation, and author of the classic book *Applied Imagination*-developed the following guidelines for generating ideas.[1] You might recognize them as Osborn's group creativity technique brainstorming:

1. *Defer judgment.* Criticism is ruled out; adverse judgment of ideas must be withheld until later.
2. *Strive for quantity.* The greater the number of ideas, the greater the likelihood of developing useful ideas.
3. *Welcome "freewheeling."* The wilder the idea, the better. It is easier to tame down than to think up.
4. *Seek combination and improvement.* How can the ideas of others be turned into better ideas? How can two or more ideas be fused into still another idea?

All of these guidelines for brainstorming are critical. Let's look at each one.

ONE: DEFER JUDGMENT

Deferring judgment is the most important guideline to keep in mind when generating ideas. But deferring judgment asks us to unlearn some of the usual ways we have been taught to think. From a very early age we learned that as soon as we thought of an idea, we needed to judge whether it was right or wrong, good or bad, safe or unsafe. But in generating new ideas and new ways to solve problems, we must hold off our judgment for a time until we have a number of ideas to choose from.

Ideas Are Not Action

One of my biggest challenges in teaching people to defer judgment and generate ideas is that they confuse ideas with action. An idea is just that, an idea; it is not an action. An idea is a potential action that might be taken later, after careful evaluation. But it is not an action when it is generated. Therefore, it needn't be feared or prematurely discarded.

Think about those times when you faced a tough problem. How many ideas did you end up with when you judged your ideas as soon as you came up with them—three, five, six? Early studies conducted on Osborn's brainstorming technique found that when members of problem solving groups deferred judgment, they came up with *70 percent* more good ideas than did groups which attacked the same problem without deferring judgment.[2] When individuals followed the deferred judgment principle, they generated *90 percent* more good ideas than they did when they mixed judgment with generation.

Separating imagination from judgment when generating ideas is not a new concept. In 1788 Friedrich Schiller wrote this in a letter to a friend who complained about his inability to generate good ideas: "In the case of the creative mind, it seems to me, the intellect has withdrawn its watch-ers from the gates, and the ideas rush in pell-mell, and only then does it review and inspect the multitude.... Hence your complaints of unfruitfulness, for you reject too soon and discriminate too severely."[3]

Judgment is a powerful tool that most of us don't recognize we control. Judgment, gone amok, often controls us. Suppose it's 3:00 A.M. and you're wide awake, thinking about your business. *I'm overpricing that item. I'm under pricing that service. I'm never going to get another consulting assignment. I can't handle all the consulting work I have now.* Yes, indeed—another judgment attack. Unwarranted, disturbing, unproductive and exhausting.

How do you deal with that kind of judgment? One of the best ways is to apply the following simple formula. It works!

Belum, Baby

Without question there are some things you have to judge now. There are other things you don't have to judge now, but can judge later. And there are a few things you never have to judge at all.

The problem comes when we judge things now that we could judge later, or that we don't need to judge at all. Of course, you must judge how your product mix contributes to the bottom line; but you probably don't need to judge that new product idea just yet. And you may *never* need to judge the weather, the kind of car your neighbor drives, or another person because of their skin color or gender.

In his book *It Was On Fire When I Lay Down On It*, Robert Fulghum discussed an Indonesian word that helps us deal with the judgment dilemma.[4] The word is *belum* (pronounced bayloom) and it means, "not quite yet." It's a wonderful word that implies continuing possibility.

"Do you speak English?"

"Belum" (not quite yet).

"Do you have any children?"

"Belum."

"Do you know the meaning of life?"

"Belum."

According to Fulghum, this word can lead to some interesting conversations and some funny moments.

"Is the taxi on fire?"

"Belum" (not quite yet).

"Have you lost ten pounds on your diet?"

"Belum."

"Do you exercise three times a week?"

"Belum."

Belum takes the edge off the harsh judgments we often make prematurely. It is a much softer approach that allows us to consider possibilities, to ponder what might be.

"Should we move into that new market?"

"Belum."

"Must we make a decision on this idea right now?"

"Belum" (not quite yet).

Take control of your judgment. Use it as a tool to help you, not as something that controls you. Separate your imaginative thinking from your judgmental thinking when generating ideas. Realize that ideas are not action. Recognize those times when you need to judge and when you can judge later. And don't be afraid to say "belum" once in a while.

Like Chess Pieces

When you consider several possible avenues of action, you should remember that daring ideas are like chess pieces moved forward; they may be beaten, but they often start a winning game.

In my capacity as leader, I'm constantly taking action and making decisions. Very often I already have an idea in mind of what I want to do in both my professional and my personal life. The danger is that I will close myself off to new opportunities because they don't fit in with my preconceived notions.

When I consciously practice deferring judgment, I create the space that encourages the people around me to voice their ideas and opinions. When I do this, very often the solution that develops is much better than anything I had thought of or was holding on to.

Robert Eckert focuses on the importance of deferring judgment when he does marriage counseling. "In most of the marriage therapy I've done," he says, "I have found that everybody needs help with learning how to shut up and listen instead of immediately judging the other person's point and developing a defense. It is almost impossible to listen when you are planning your defense or attack strategy."[5]

When you consciously refrain from judging ideas, you begin to open up entirely new vistas; you weren't able to see them because you were judging so severely. When you defer judgment, you open yourself to the infinite possibilities before you. And success moves that much closer to your reach.

TWO: STRIVE FOR QUANTITY

This is a quiz.

It's Monday morning. Your boss walks into your office and says, "You know, we are having problems landing the XYZ account. Why don't we get a few people together to brainstorm this?"

Question: When your boss says "brainstorm," what does he mean?

a. You are going to discuss the problem.
b. You are going to have a gripe session.
c. You are going to review three or four things you've done in the past.
d. You are going to sit and listen to the boss's ideas and tell him how good they are.
e. None of the above.

Answer: "E," none of the above.

Let's look at our quiz again and consider some of the replies. First, a brainstorming session is not a group discus-

sion. Very specific guidelines are required to effectively generate ideas in a brainstorming session. Early brainstorming
research found that those groups which followed specific
guidelines for generating ideas came up with more and better
ideas.

Second, a brainstorming session is absolutely *not* a
gripe session. In a properly conducted brainstorming session,
the problem is well–defined and the group focuses on generating ideas to solve that problem. The idea is to generate potential ideas for action, not complaints.

Third, a brainstorming session is not dreaming up three
or four ideas and then discussing them. Sometimes when I
start to work with a new company, my client makes it a point
to tell me about the brainstorming sessions his group con-
ducts. I then ask him, "How many ideas do your people come
up with in these sessions?"

"Oh, usually five or six," he replies.

Wrong! That's not brainstorming.

The more ideas you generate, the greater are your
chances of coming up with good ideas. An effective brainstorming session is not generating four ideas in five minutes; it
is generating forty ideas in five minutes!

To get that kind of quantity, it is helpful to set an idea
quota for the session. Forty ideas in five minutes is not unreasonable for a trained group.

So, how many ideas do you have to come up with to get
a good one? Do you have to come up with hundreds of ideas
to generate one good candidate? It all depends on the kinds of
ideas you want.

If you want to find ways to improve your current methods, you will need fewer ideas than if your goal is to completely
redefine the nature of your business or your life. If you want to
break out of your current patterns and create some major
breakthroughs, then you will need significantly more ideas
than if you want to make some incremental improvement on
an existing process or procedure.

Unfortunately, we can't precisely predict the number of
ideas you will need; but setting a quota or goal for ideas generated helps. Between forty to fifty ideas is a good quota if you
want to generate ideas to improve your current methods. More

than fifty ideas will help you begin to really stretch your thinking, but if you want to completely redefine the work you are doing and create some exotic ways to approach a problem, a quota of 100 ideas or more is not unreasonable. I've found that in sessions where hundreds of ideas are generated, the last 20 percent really begin to "push the envelope."

Provide a Clear Target

But why use an idea quota in the first place? The main reason is to stretch the group beyond the five or six ideas that are usually generated. Also, instead of continually trying to persuade a group to generate more and more ideas, a quota provides a clear target.

I'm sure some of you are wondering: *Okay, bottom line it for me. Are quantity and quality really related? If I conduct a brainstorming session and come up with a bunch of crazy ideas, how do I know I will get any good ones?*

Several years ago my colleagues and I conducted a study at the Center for Studies in Creativity at Buffalo State College in Buffalo, New York, on this very question.[6] We compared twenty groups of students trained in the use of Creative Problem Solving techniques with twenty student groups that did not receive this training. We presented the groups with a specific business problem and asked them to solve it. We found that the groups trained to use CPS outproduced the untrained groups by a ratio of about three to one on quantity of ideas.

But were those extra ideas any good? When business experts evaluated the ideas for quality, they found that the groups trained in CPS out-performed their counterparts by a margin of more than two to one. The final result: 618 ideas rated as excellent in the trained groups, compared to 281 excellent ideas in the untrained groups.

More Is Merrier

That's the laboratory application—but what about real life? How will this information help you to top your competition, add more to the bottom line, and increase employee productivity? A 1993 study in *Total Employee Involvement Newsletter* entitled, "U.S./Japan Suggestion-System Report: Bigger Ain't

Better; More Is Merrier," reported the following benefit of generating many ideas.[7]

> There are two ways to score in baseball: hit a home run, or combine a bunt, hit-and-run and sacrifice fly. The second involves more players, along with the coaching staff. Yet our annual comparison of suggestion-system statistics from the Japan Human Relations Association and the Employee Involvement Association indicates that most American companies still swing for the fences. This, despite compelling evidence that bottom-line wins go to companies with systems akin to the Total Improvement Proposal System which encourages greater participation, lots of ideas, and small but meaningful awards.

In this study, Japanese employees submitted an average of 32.5 ideas per worker, with an implementation rate of 88 percent. Contrast this to U.S. workers who submitted an average of 0.17 ideas per worker annually, with an implementation rate of 37 percent.

The study continued,

> American companies reaped more savings per implemented idea and doled out larger awards. But the bigger bottom-line boost comes with many small ideas, not a few large ones. Japanese companies have a 22 fold advantage in net savings per 100 eligible employees.[8]

Total Employee Involvement used the following table to illustrate this dramatic comparison.[9]

Suggestion System Data Category	U.S.	Japan
Eligible Employees	6,796,506	1,749,659
Suggestions received	1,170,122	56,966,011
Suggestions per 100 eligible employees	17	3255
Participation rate	8%	73.6%
Adoption rate	37%	88.7%
Average award per adoption	$510.67	$3.20
Average net savings per adoption	$6,405	$197
Net savings per 100 eligible employees	$30,261	$683,753.*

*Based on $1.00 U.S. =Yen 126

Those statistics look pretty dismal don't they? The article provided some hope. It stated:

> Several companies operating in America—notably Japanese transplants such as Honda of America, Nippondenso, and Toyota prove that motivated American workers can deliver incremental improvements that result in bottom-line cost savings, not to mention breakthrough ideas that often arise from small innovations.
>
> Beyond the Japanese transplants, the data point to other companies enlisting a majority of their workforce to make improvements. Siemens Industrial Auto, received about 8.5 ideas from each eligible worker and boasted a 99% participation rate with an average award of $3.76. Parker Hannifin-Nichols received 2.25 ideas per employee with a 98% participation rate, while paying an average award of $12.33.
>
> But there is still plenty of business as usual. LTV Steel company received the U.S. average 0.17 ideas per employee with a 12% participation rate. Although the company implemented a respectable 45% of ideas submitted, it paid awards as large as $67,000. Each eligible Pitney Bowes employee contributed a mere 0.05 suggestions, and only 4% participated. Yet the company paid an average award of $362.[10]

The large awards doled out to employees in American companies actually seemed to inhibit the idea suggestion process. The article continued, "Many employees seem daunted by large awards, thinking perhaps that their contribution has to be huge to be worth anything. It's as if these companies are saying, 'If you can't hit homers, don't bother coming to bat.'"

THE AMERICAN CREATIVITY MYTH

A pernicious myth in American culture states that the only way to be creative is to come up with a breakthrough that no one ever dreamed of, an idea that conventional wisdom said was impossible. Such a break-through, of course, must radically change the world as we know it—as did the Wright flyer, Alexander Graham Bell's telephone, and Edison's light bulb.

The American view of creativity is the big hit, the home run, the big bang, the instant profit. But creativity is not only the big breakthrough; creativity is also improving, refining, and reshaping ideas already in existence.

Have you ever considered what would have happened if the three breakthroughs mentioned above had never been improved or refined? To most people a 747 doesn't seem as creative as the Wright's airplane. After all, it's not sexy, flashy or brand-new; it merely represents incremental improvements that accrued over time.

This home-run view of creativity has been extremely detrimental to American business and is often threatening to leaders. Did you know that fax machine technology was invented in the United States? It was never taken to market because the short-term costs of making it commercially viable were prohibitive. Today it is rare to find an office in America that does not have a fax machine, and many people have them in their homes. None of the machines, however, are made in the United States; all are made in Japan or other Pacific Rim countries. It was the Japanese who took the long view and improved facsimile technology to make it profitable.

Video technology also was invented in the United States, yet it was also too expensive to develop and market in a short period. Today most American households have at least one, sometimes two VCRs-but none are made by American companies, and only one firm, Quasar, manufactures VCRs in this country (Quasar is owned by Panasonic, a Japanese corporation!).

So what's the real problem? Is it American impatience? Is it our short-term, quarterly-profit mentality? Is it

continued on page 77

continued on page 77
leadership's demands for instant results? While those suggestions cover part of the problem, the real culprit is our view of creativity. We need to remind ourselves that while home runs are important, more games are won with a series of singles than with a round-tripper.

As a leader, you need to pay attention to both small and big ideas. Remember, if you never give the little idea a chance, you will never get those multi-million dollar big hits.

This is dangerous news. If you never give the little idea a chance, you never get the multi-million dollar breakthrough ideas. By encouraging and rewarding people for the small, incremental improvement ideas, you support the process of idea generation and train people to contribute ideas. Employees begin to trust the process when they contribute ideas and see results. When people trust the process and see that their ideas are not going to be rejected, they will contribute more ideas, often riskier ideas, ideas that break the current paradigm and create breakthroughs. You never know when the big breakthrough is going to occur, so you need to pay attention to all the ideas. Additionally, thousands of incremental improvements, over time, create significantly greater improvement than one big, short-term hit.

Masaaki Imai, author of the book Kaizen ("improvement" in Japanese), concluded that one of the outstanding features of Japanese management is that it generates a great number of suggestions from workers.[11] Management works hard to consider these suggestions and often incorporates them into the overall Kaizen strategy. Using this approach, the input for continuous improvement comes from the entire system, not just a few supervisors or managers.

Studies show that highly competitive organizations effectively take advantage of this human resource to fuel the continuous process of change and improvement. These organizations are constantly looking to find new ways of doing things better, whether the change involves an executive job or work at any level throughout the organization.

Consider your own business. What's the first step in getting a lot of sales? Answer: Have a lot of prospects. Think of ideas as prospects, prospects for new ways to solve the problem. Just as a lot of prospects will lead to a lot of sales, a lot of ideas will lead to breakthroughs. And what's the best way to get a lot of prospects? Generate a lot of ideas about where to find them. The more ideas, the more potential prospects—and the more successful you will be.

THREE: WELCOME FREEWHEELING
What do you think of the following two pronouncements?

> "Everything that can be invented has been invented."
> Charles H. Duell, Director of the United States
> Patent Office, 1899

> "Who the hell wants to hear actors talk?"
> Harry Warner, Warner Brothers' Pictures

The remarks appear terribly shortsighted, don't they? They suggest the lack of ability to freewheel, to dream up new ideas and concepts, to imagine what might be instead of focusing on what is. They also indicate a desire to hang on to the status quo instead of building toward the future.

The More Unusual, The Better
Freewheeling encourages us to generate unusual ideas and emphasizes that it is easier to tame down a wild idea than it is to invigorate a weak one. When working with various groups, from students in my classes to corporate presidents, I've found that freewheeling is one of the most difficult idea-generating guidelines to apply.

This is particularly true when groups are working on a problem that is important to them. When I ask members of a brainstorming group how many wild ideas they've come up with, they generally respond, "This is a serious problem. We can't do something outlandish."

But look closely at that statement. I asked about the *ideas* they generated, not the *actions* they're planning to take. Again, it's the problem of confusing ideas with action. The purpose of a brainstorming session is to generate ideas—just ideas—not to take action. Ideas become actions only when you take the time to select, develop, refine, and then do something with them. There is a time for selecting and refining ideas; but at the idea generation phase, absolutely anything goes. When you are generating ideas, don't worry if your ideas seem outlandish, far-fetched, or even foolish. It may well be that one of these "outlandish" ideas becomes the core of a major breakthrough.

Why Is It So Difficult?
So why is it so difficult for people to freewheel and come up with wild concepts? One of the reasons is that many of us unconsciously block any idea that appears unusual or which deviates from standard procedure. We have a set pattern for solving problems and are reluctant to deviate from what we have already predetermined are the acceptable answers.

Here is the unfortunate paradox: We resist accepting ideas that don't fit our established pattern, but the reason for conducting a CPS session is to search for new ways to solve a problem in which all of our previously acceptable ideas have failed!

Another reason why it is difficult for us to freewheel is that many of us don't work in a trusting environment in which we feel comfortable sharing our ideas. We want to remain safe and not appear silly or foolish.

One of the benefits of having the courage to practice freewheeling in a brainstorming group is that by sharing your wild ideas you show that you trust the other members of the group. The risk you take toward establishing this trust helps the creative process develop and build.

FOUR: SEEK COMBINATION AND IMPROVEMENT
The technique of Combination and Improvement is also known as building. In addition to contributing ideas of their own, participants should suggest how the ideas of others can be turned into better ideas, or how two or more ideas can be joined into still another idea. Building occurs when problem solvers add to or improve the ideas generated by others in the group. Building happens almost naturally in a smoothly functioning brainstorming session.
CHECK YOUR EGO AT THE DOOR

To allow building to occur, it is important to leave your ego out of an idea generating session. When your ego begins to attach itself to an idea that you contributed, you will be less likely to want others to improve your idea. You will also want to claim that idea in later stages of the process. When I interview people who have participated in a highly productive brainstorming session, most don't even recall which ideas they contributed and who built on those ideas.

Building is crucial. The Wright brothers were the first to effectively control heavier-than-air powered flight, but what would have happened if no one built on that idea? Would you rather fly in a Wright flyer or a 747?

Closely related to building ideas is reinforcing that it is perfectly acceptable to repeat ideas in an idea generating session. Often people in my sessions will censor or refuse to record ideas that occur a second time. But this is counterproductive.

Ideas generated in various phases of an idea generating session, even though they might appear to be identical, can actually have different meanings. For example, if an idea comes up at number 12 and someone repeats the same idea at number 22, is it the same idea? Answer: No. Ten ideas have been generated since the idea first appeared and number 22 exists in a different context. The context in which an idea exists determines how we perceive the idea and the meaning it carries. Ten ideas later, this idea might have a different meaning.

Also, by failing to record the repeated ideas, you lose the overall quality of the session. Ideas are reappearing for a reason. Often, when groups go back and review the ideas they generated, the repeated ideas form themes or clusters. These idea clusters are often indicators of solutions the group needs to implement.

SUCCESS IN PACKAGING DESIGN

Remarkable results can be achieved when these elements of CPS are carefully implemented. According to Jeff Harris, Senior Engineer in the packaging dynamics laboratory for The Clorox Company, breakthroughs can occur even in a field as specialized as designing packaging to ship consumer products.

In designing packaging for a product, it is essential to look for cost savings, since packaging adds costs to products. If you can reduce the amount of money spent for packing a product, you can essentially increase profits.

Jeff was able to reduce the cost to package a product from $7.64 to $3.27. (By the way, the packaging design that cost $7.64 failed; the package allowed its contents to sustain damage.) Here's how Jeff improved the quality and reliability of the packaging through his application of Creative Problem Solving.

When Jeff was transferred from his work of fifteen years as an analytical chemist to the protective packaging area, Clorox sent him to a training program on packaging design. Here's what happened next:

> It was an outside training class, a generic program, and I was sent as an introduction to the process of packaging design. Our objective was to design a protective package for a specialty computer. It had a part that was subject to breakage in the distribution environment (UPS or Federal Express).
>
> Over-packaging in this case was responsible for the product failures in the field. Excessive packing amplified the vibrations from riding in an 18 wheel tractor-trailer rig across the country and damaged the computer.
>
> We were divided into teams to work on this problem. Some of the teams jumped immediately to trying to find the cause; they didn't spend any time trying to agree on a problem statement.
>
> I think some of the training I've received in creativity and innovation helped protect me in the sense that other participants in the workshop used "killer phrases" (judgmental terms) when ideas were generated. I "put my armor on" and looked at things from a different perspective. I tried to find more than one right answer.
>
> Some of the folks in the course didn't look for more than one right answer. When they found one "right answer," they stopped. I continued to look at options

that might be more radical and tried to change the paradigm a bit. Of course, the more radical the approach, the more likely one will have a breakthrough-and in this case, it would be a huge cost savings.

In the workshop, we had to work with a material that had never been used in packaging design. People looked at it and said, "Well, the static stress is ten times too high." Also, this material was delivered in a certain format, either a four-inch block or a four-inch sheet. When other participants looked at the material they would say, "Well, the weight of the computer doesn't justify its use; it's out of line." And they would discard it. And I would say, "No, what that means to me is that I can use only one-tenth of the amount and achieve the same thing. The static stress will then be in line with what I need to protect the computer, from an environmental standpoint."[12]

When Jeff proposed using this material in this particular design, his ideas did not win immediate acceptance.

Some people don't act like team members. They fold their arms and send the signal that they are not going to put any energy into the idea because they "know" the idea won't work. There was one fellow in this group from a very innovative company who spent more time discrediting other people than congratulating them. So I decided I wasn't going to be meek and modest; I was going to be a warrior if I had to. That's what "putting on the suit of armor" is all about. It is not letting people get to you, even if they are throwing lots of killer phrases.

Anyway, we tested the idea. There were still some folks who said it would not work and didn't want to go along with it. But once the initial tests showed it was possible, everyone got on board.[13]

When I asked Jeff what made this breakthrough successful, he mentioned four things.

1. He took the time to redefine the problem. He didn't

accept the problem as it was initially proposed.

s2. He looked for more than one right answer to solve the
   problem. He didn't stop when he came up with his first solution.

3. He intentionally tried to challenge the traditionally accepted paradigm of packaging with a different material.

4. When killer phrases came his way, he "put on his armor" and didn't let those phrases get him down.[14]

Those who use Creative Problem Solving to break through to new ideas which add directly to a company's bottom line aren't always commended or even appreciated. But in the end, the payoff can be startling.

I mean, would you rather take a call from a customer who received his computer intact and fully functioning, or from some screamer who keeps bellowing about a machine that arrived in piles of shiny pieces?

I trust you get my point.

SIX
How to Conduct an Idea-Generating Session

Ideas awaken each other ... .
because they have always been related.
DENIS DIDEROT
Laughing at a wild idea discourages the flow of ideas,
and in particular, the individual who suggested it.
J. G. RAWLINSON

A forge plant in upstate New York makes ring gears for cars. Now, a ring gear is not a very glamorous product, but it is very important when you are making cars. Ring gears change the flow of power from one direction to another. Ring gears go in your car's rear axle on rear wheel drive cars or the transaxle in front wheel drive cars. This plant sells ring gears to General Motors, Toyota, Saturn, and other automobile manufacturers.

Ring gears are made by taking a super-hot piece of metal and putting it into a die. The die is then stamped with about twenty tons of pressure. A hot piece of metal goes in one side and a hot piece of metal in the shape of a ring gear comes out the other. Trouble occurs, however, when the ring gear gets stuck in the die. When a ring gear gets stuck in the die, the machine operator has to use a tool that looks like a crowbar to break the ring gear loose from the die. Most of the time when this happened, the operator broke the ring gear, creating a quality problem. Operators were also starting to break the dies. With dies costing anywhere from five thousand to ten thousand dollars apiece and operators breaking from three to five dies a week, the company had a big problem.

The people in this plant were being trained in

Creative Problem Solving. We asked them to work on goals, wishes, challenges, or problems that were important to them, and the group on this particular day decided to work on the problem of: "How might we prevent the ring gear from sticking in the die?" This plant was also working to train cross-functional teams, so in this training session were a number of people from different parts of the organization. Machine operators were accompanied by managers, sales people, secretaries, engineers, and chemists.

Nathan Bliss, United Auto Workers Education and Problem Solving Training Coordinator, made the following remarks about the results the people in his organization achieved through applying Creative Problem Solving:

> We've had tremendous amounts of fun in using Creative Problem Solving. One of the concerns we were having was metal sticking in the die that we use to forge ring gears. So, one of the operators took a big swab of grease and put it in the die. Later we found out that the grease was holding scale. This caused a build-up in the die and after several parts, the die broke. In one of our Creative Problem Solving sessions we were generating ideas to deal with this sticking problem. We identified the problem as, "How might we prevent the ring gears from sticking in the die?" We started generating ideas but then started to slow down. So the individual who was facilitating the session tried the Forced Connections technique and asked the question, "How can we use something that doesn't fit with this problem at all?"
>
> One of the participants came up with the idea of spraying the die with the vegetable product PAM. "It prevents sticking when my wife sprays it on her pans," he said. The whole group laughed, but the PAM idea got one of the other participants thinking. "I'm not sure if PAM will work or not, but some number ten soap and Pen Field oil 108 mixed together just might."
>
> Several members of the group got a spray bottle that cost one dollar. They mixed some of the solution

that was readily available in the plant. At the beginning of each shift, the operators sprayed the solution on the die. This solution lubricated the die and, as a result, there haven't been any sticking problems since and we haven't had any broken dies."[1]

The result: A solution sprayed on the die costs about twenty-five cents, the bottle about $1.00. This $1.25 solution is regularly saving the plant anywhere from $5,000 to $40,000 dollars a week.

Is it realistic for you to expect to experience dramatic results like this every time you hold a Creative Problem Solving session? I'd love to say yes, but the answer is No. The catch is, you never know when such phenomenal rewards might occur. Yet by implementing ideas that create incremental improvement in the organization, you increase organizational members' confidence in their creative ability and set the stage for those big breakthroughs.

NO FUNNY FACES

Before we get to some specific ways of generating many ideas, let's cover a couple of essential basics. The first has to do with criticism.

When generating ideas, don't criticize your ideas or the ideas of others. Remain open to all possibilities. This, of course, means no sarcasm. Don't make funny faces at other peoples' ideas. Get involved in the session and positively support what is happening. Leaders and supervisors must set an example of what they expect. Your people are watching you very closely!

It is helpful to set a time limit of ten to fifteen minutes when generating ideas. Most people can hold off their judgment for that amount of time. After the time limit is up, or when some workable solutions to the problem have been generated, *then* you can evaluate the ideas. But *do not* try to generate and evaluate ideas at the same time.

WHEN YOU GET STUCK FOR IDEAS, LOOK AROUND

Anytime you try to generate a lot of ideas during a Creative Problem Solving Session, there is the very real possibility that you will bog down. You should expect that a time will come when it will seem as if you're running out of gas. The question is, how do you consciously get yourself out of your self-imposed ruts? Answer: Look around.

Consider this scenario. You're in the middle of a high-powered, fast-paced idea generating session. Your group is following the rules for brain-storming to the letter. No one is criticizing ideas. You have set a quota for at least 80 ideas. Some wonderfully farfetched ideas are being generated. People are building on ideas as fast as high performance race cars in the Indianapolis 500.

Then suddenly it happens. You stop. The well runs dry. You hit a rut. You and the members of your group sit around the conference table and stare at each other. The unthinkable has happened. You've run out of ideas! What do you do? Don't worry-there is a way out of this.

THE FORCED CONNECTIONS TECHNIQUE
One tool to help you get out of the idea-generating doldrums is a technique called forced connections. Forced connections work like this: Take the problem you are trying to solve. Pick an object or a situation from a completely unrelated area and make a connection or find a relationship between the two situations. The result of this connection is a new idea.

Suppose you're trying to improve the way information is communicated in your company. Things are happening so quickly in your business that your people can't seem to keep up with what's going on. So you decide to conduct an idea-generating session on the problem. This time, instead of being overtaken by inertia, you look around the room and notice the fresh cheese Danish you are about to devour. You try forcing a connection between your cheese Danish and the communication problem. As you make your forced connection, you might come up with some of the following ideas:

★ Put updated company information in little capsules
   that people eat with their morning coffee
★ Break the information down into bite-sized pieces

      that people can read on their lunch breaks
  ✶ Write company information on napkins and have
     them distributed with everyone's morning coffee
  ✶ Play a videotape in the cafeteria during lunch and
     breaks that features updated company information

There, you've done it! You've climbed out of the idea rut
and are moving again.

Forced connections are based on the principle that
one of the best ways to create new ideas is to combine old
ideas in a new way. Some of the most interesting and valuable ideas we have are the result of this idea-connecting
process. Gutenberg's invention of the printing press is a
wonderful example of a forced connection.

At the beginning of the fifteenth century, printing was
no longer a novelty in Europe. Wooden blocks were
engraved in relief with pictures or text. The blocks were
then thoroughly wetted with a brown pigment-like substance. A sheet of damp paper was laid on the block and
the back of the paper was rubbed with a dauber or burnisher until an impression of the carved relief was transferred to it. Each sheet of paper could be printed on only
one side—a cumbersome process at best.

Gutenberg's goal was to print the Bible, but it was
useless to think of engraving all thirteen hundred pages on
pieces of wood. At that time Gutenberg already had a crude
form of movable type. He could cast individual letters in the
form of coins or seals (similar to the ones used to make
impressions in wax on the back of an envelope). Yet if
Gutenberg cast his individual letters in the form of seals,
the seals would shift as he rubbed paper over them. He
could never make a clear print using the traditional
method.

He tried everything under the sun, but nothing presented itself. Finally he took a break and went to a nearby
wine festival to sample the latest vintage. He wrote, "I
watched the wine flowing, and going back from the effect to
the cause, I studied the power of the wine press which
nothing can resist."

GET YOUR PICTURES *NOW*

It's important to bring a childlike perspective to your problem. A great example of this is the story of the Polaroid-Land camera. In 1943 Edwin Land took his three-year-old daughter, Jennifer, for a before-Christmas vacation near Santa Fe, New Mexico. They spent one day taking pictures with Land's Rolleiflex camera. At the end of the day, they sat down in front of a roaring fire at their cottage. Land and Jennifer began to talk about their day—how they took pictures of a burro delivering firewood, of the local cathedral, of Indian women selling jewelry, and some pictures of Jennifer. At that moment Jennifer asked, "Why can't I see the pictures *now?*"

It was that naive and innocent question that got Land thinking and eventually led to the development of the Polaroid camera—an invention that does, indeed, allow you to see your pictures almost instantly.

Land was so taken by the value of the child-like perspective on a problem that for years after this incident, children regularly visited the research labs at Polaroid and were encouraged to roam freely and ask scientists all kinds of questions about their work. Land wanted his scientists to have access to fresh views of the problems they were tackling. He never forgot that it was a childlike view that created his multi-million dollar business.

At that moment it occurred to him that the same steady pressure the wine press exerts on grapes might be applied to his seals on paper. Eureka! With a few modifications, the printing press was born.

Now, it seems a pretty big stretch from drinking wine to printing manuscripts, or from the wine press to the printing press. But if you look at the history of creativity and new ideas, it is often this conjoining of ideas from completely different worlds that creates powerful new concepts.

The microwave oven is a more recent invention that illustrates this stretching from one world to another. Microwaves are used to transmit telephone conversations, satellite television transmissions, and for police radar. They belong to the same family that radio, television, and radar waves do. Microwaves are reflected by metals, similar to the way light is reflected by mirrors. At the proper wavelength, when microwaves are confined in an enclosed space, like a metal box, they can quickly increase temperatures in food, water, and other substances. Voila! Lunch! The same technology that can be used to communicate over long distances can be used to cook your food. From communication to cooking, another big leap between concepts occurs.

A LITTLE EXERCISE

Practice deferring judgment by trying this exercise. Set aside a weekend in which you refuse to judge those that are close to you. When you find yourself judging, just remind yourself not to judge. Instead, just listen. *Refuse* to judge. Sometimes you will find yourself screaming to yourself not to judge, but as the weekend progresses, you will find it easier.

Can't refrain from judging for a whole weekend? Then try it for a day or half a day or even an hour. Think about it: You have been judging these people who are close to you probably from the first moment you met them. So take a vacation from judging!

Your next challenge: Don't judge at a business meeting. Or if that is too difficult, don't judge the first ten ideas that come out on the table. You might break a pencil or two in marking down the number of ideas you're letting go by without judging, but it will be money well spent. Pencils are replaceable; some ideas aren't.

So what's the recipe for creating forced connections? If you find yourself slowing down in an idea-generating session, simply look around the room and make a connection or force a relationship between the problem and another object. The idea you generate by using the forced connection technique might not be the breakthrough you need—it might even seem ridiculous—but it may well help you get the flow of ideas started again.

Catalogs with photographs are excellent sources for creating forced connections. When you find yourself slowing down, pick an item at random from the catalog and see if you can relate it to your problem. Don't worry if the first few ideas you create are ridiculous; the others that follow could be the breakthrough you are searching for.

The yellow pages also work well for forced connections. Just flip open the phone book and "let your fingers do the walking" through the many categories listed. Look for something as far away from your problem as possible. If you are working on an office problem, don't zero in on office equipment.

Forced connections is not merely a group technique. Use it when you are working by yourself to generate ideas. Just remember, the greater the stretch between worlds, the more novel and unique the ideas you will create. So let yourself go and see what wonderful new ideas you can invent!

GETTING STARTED

So how do you do an idea-generating session? How do you generate those breakthrough ideas? What are the specific behaviors for running a CPS session? The following suggestions are designed for those leaders who want to facilitate creative problem solving sessions.

First, practice is essential for effective use of Creative Problem Solving. Great sport teams practice. Great symphony orchestras practice. Fire departments and emergency rescue teams practice. They practice so that when they must perform at peak effectiveness under extremely stressful conditions, they can execute extremely well.

Question: When do we practice team problem solving? Answer: Usually, we don't. Too often we wait for a problem to hit and only then do we try to solve it-at the same time trying to work out the process for doing so. Such a practice, of course, is extremely ineffective, time consuming, and usually results in half-baked, poor solutions. What would happen if the rescue squad that arrived to save you after a car accident had to figure out who was going to do what and how they were going to do it? Would you like to be their test case? Neither would I.

Now, just imagine what would happen if the next

time a problem confronted your business, you knew exactly how to go about solving that problem. And further imagine that you trusted the process because you had practiced it and used it successfully. Is that a more pleasant thought? I think so, too.

CPS SESSION ROLES
Clearly defined roles are one of the most important aspects when applying Creative Problem Solving in a group, just as clearly defined roles are essential for a rescue squad and a sports team. There are three essential roles for an effective CPS session: client, facilitator, and resource group.

One: Client
The person who owns the challenge and has primary decision-making authority on how it is to be dealt with is the client. Sometimes an entire team owns the challenge and all the members share the client role. This role can be very tricky for leaders, because many times it is the leader who owns the challenge, and it is the leader who often leads the meeting. The person who owns the challenge is probably the worst person to facilitate the session.

If you are the leader, and you want to apply Creative Problem Solving to your challenge, then here are a couple of important suggestions. First, make sure that you and your team are well trained in Creative Problem Solving. Next, make sure there are several people in your organization who have some additional facilitation training. so they can conduct the session, and you, as the leader, can be freed up to make your contributions without having to worry about managing the process.

Two: Facilitator
Use the facilitator to manage the CPS process and keep the group moving toward a successful resolution to the challenge. The facilitator is not involved in the actual content of the session. The facilitator can be a member of your work group who doesn't have a stake in the challenge or someone from outside your group. As I mentioned, the facilitator generally shouldn't be the team leader. But it is crucial that

the leader is part of the group to provide support and assure that action will be taken on the outcome.

If the facilitator is recording all the ideas on a chart, and not using the Brainstorming with Post-its technique (explained on page 95), it is important that the facilitator write down all the ideas as they are spoken. The facilitator should not change, modify or try to "improve" the idea. Changes, modifications, or the facilitator's attempt to improve an idea are forms of judgment and will stifle the generation of ideas.

Three: Resource Group
The people who generate options or ideas to help deal effectively with the challenge are the members of the resource group. These individuals are trained in the CPS procedures discussed in this book. I recommend that some of the resource group members be well versed in the problem on which the group is working, but it is also helpful to have some people in the group who are not familiar with the problem at all. It is these people who bring a fresh perspective to the situation. These are the people who don't know what can't be done. They are not aware of the previous methods that have been applied to the problem, that may or may not have worked, and therefore don't have those mental blocks.

WARMING UP TO BE CREATIVE
It might be helpful to compare a CPS session to a team sport or any sort of physical exercise. Just as you warm up for physical activity, it is also important to warm up for mental activity. Before applying Creative Problem Solving to a work-related problem, practice the idea-generating methods with a challenge the group can enjoy and on which they can experience some success.

Some ideal "warm up" exercises include generating ideas for the perfect bathtub; generating ideas for using ten million Ping-Pong balls; and generating other uses for common objects like a chair, a brick, a basketball, or a plunger. It is helpful to have a picture or a sample of the object available for participants.

In the warm-up session, set a time limit of five minutes and a quota of approximately thirty ideas. A second idea-generating session can also be conducted on the same problem; but in the second session, double the quota and have participants practice the Forced Connections technique. Conduct the practice session before you introduce the problem.

THE POST-IT NOTE BRAINSTORMING TECHNIQUE
There are several ways to do a brainstorming session. One of the easiest and most effective is called the Post-it Brainstorming technique. This method uses Post-its, a flip-chart and lots of flip chart paper. This technique makes the process move more smoothly and does not require the facilitator to write every problem statement or idea. To use the Post-it technique, each member of the resource group and the client have a 3x5 Post-it pad and a thin-line felt tip marker. When someone has something they want to contribute using this technique, the following guidelines are recommended:

1. Say your idea or problem statement when you write it. In this way, other members of the group hear your thinking. They can then build off the idea or problem statement to add more. Then hand your Post-it to the facilitator to be placed on the flip chart.
2. Write your idea or problem statement large and legibly enough to be read by the group.
3. One idea or problem statement per Post-it.
4. When generating ideas, keep your ideas direct and to the point. Think of writing your idea as you would write a newspaper headline. After you are done generating ideas, you can go back and clarify the idea further. Members of the group can ask a brief question, but be careful not to turn the idea-generating session into a discussion of each idea. The items can be discussed after you have finished generating.

PLAN THE SESSION LOGISTICS

Make sure that all the necessary equipment and support materials are assembled for the Brainstorming with Post-its session. The flip chart should have plenty of paper and each person should have a Post-it pad and a felt-tip marker. Provide any visuals that are necessary and have a few items for the forced connections technique available. Make sure the room you are working in is comfortable and the participants will not be disturbed. If there is a phone in the room, turn it off. Avoid any unnecessary interruptions.

THE BRAINWRITING TECHNIQUE

In addition to using the Brainstorming with Post-its technique, you can also use a technique called Brainwriting.[2] When a group uses Brainwriting, members do not have to talk to each other. Each person writes their ideas down on a Brainwriting form like the one shown on page 97.

The Brainwriting technique offers several unique benefits. Because people are writing their ideas down on a form, they don't have to talk to each other. That gives people who might be reluctant to talk in a Brainstorming session the opportunity to express their ideas. Second, if someone is dominating the session and spewing out ideas without giving others a chance to contribute, brainwriting gives everyone a chance to participate.

Sometimes people might be reluctant to contribute ideas because their boss is in the session and they might not want to appear foolish. Because people are writing their ideas down instead of saying them outloud-unless the boss is a handwriting analyst-the contributions are relatively anonymous. Additionally, more ideas can be generated because people don't have to say their idea when they write it and then hand it up to a facilitator to place on a flip chart.

Finally, because people are contributing individually, the participants in the idea-generating session do not have to be in the same place at the same time to generate ideas. Brainwriting forms can be faxed to different locations with everyone contributing an idea. The form can also be adapted for e-mail systems.

BRAINWRITING

Problem statement:_____

_____

1A	1B	1C
2A	2B	2C
3A	3B	3C

CONDUCTING A BRAINWRITING SESSION

To conduct a Brainwriting session, make sure each person in the group has a Brainwriting Form, with several extra forms in the middle of the work area. Follow the guidelines for generating ideas:

1. Defer judgment
2. Strive for quantity
3. Freewheel (the wilder the idea the better)
4. Seek combinations and improvement (build on ideas)

To begin a Brainwriting session, write the problem statement at the top of the form in the "problem statement" space, beginning with the words "How to . . . ?" "How might I . . . ?" or "In what ways might I ... ?" Then write three ideas across the top row (Ideas 1 A, 1B, and IC).

As soon as you have written three ideas, place the form in the middle of the work area and pick up a form someone else has completed. Don't continue on the form you have just used.

The first person to put the Brainwriting form in the middle should pick up and write ideas on an extra form. With extra forms in the middle, you will not have to wait for other members of the group to finish. A form will always be waiting for you!

Write three more ideas across the second row (Ideas 2A, 2B, and 2C). These can be ideas you have just thought of or ideas stimulated by the ones already written down. These ideas can also be builds, refinements, or modifications of the ideas that are already on the form.

Eventually, your Brainwriting form might come back to you. Just make sure that there are not more than three of your ideas together. Generate many different ideas and possibilities. Think: *Three ideas and go! Three ideas and go!*

BRIGHTENING UP PAPER AT MEAD

I know that to some business executives, the techniques and ideas we've just outlined seem far removed from the bottom line. They may keep employees happy for a little while, but they don't really help the company beat its competitors.

One word of caution: Don't try to convince David Newcomer of that.

David is head of Mead Fine Papers' Papeterie

Marketing group. His group applied Creative Problem Solving to enhance the brightness and shade of Mead's greeting card papers, thus creating a competitive edge in the process. Mead had been struggling for years to achieve the levels of brightness in its premium papeterie grades that equaled its competitor's product. But let's allow David to tell the story, which I've used here with his permission:

> In our industry, quality is often a function of "brightness." We want as much light reflected from the surface of the paper as possible. For example, if a paper could reflect 100 percent of the light off its surface, the brightness would be 100. In the past, our mill had struggled to get a sheet equal to a strong competitor's product. The competitor was producing a 95 bright product with a much nicer shade than we produced.
>
> This competitor was the backup supplier to one of our major customers, one of the country's largest greeting card manufacturers. This competitor's primary business is not making paper for greeting cards, but photographic papers. About eight years ago, when the photographic paper business got really hot, they failed to supply their greeting card customers with the bright paper. Our key greeting card company approached us and said, "We need Mead to make us a 95 bright product because the other supplier is not supplying it."
>
> Our response to that request eight years ago was, "Well, we can't either, but for different reasons. We simply can't get that bright."
>
> After much discussion, we agreed to force our system and attempted the 95 bright product. We loaded up the product with a lot of different dyes and optical brighteners and managed to get a sheet that was almost 94 bright. It turned out to have a pink shade to it and it cost us a lot to make because we were at the top of our system's limit. It wasn't very attractive but it sufficed. We were not very proud of it and lost money making it.

After our competition's photographic paper market softened, they reentered the greeting card market and began cutting prices to the point where not even the most loyal of customers was able to resist. As we began losing some of our market share, we again began to realize the need for a bright sheet. While our customers went back to the competitor, they were not happy to have to buy the product from a "fair-weather supplier." We needed a product that was economical to make, profitable to sell, and equal to any competitive product. After all, Mead is the largest manufacturer of greeting card papers in the world and we were not proud of the fact that a premium product being sold into our market had to come from someone whose primary business was elsewhere. We owed our customers more than that.

Right after we had participated in your creativity workshops down at Cabin Bluff and in Chillicothe, Ohio, the team John Becker and I had assembled selected the goal of "increasing our brightness" as our number one priority. Not being content with just matching the competition, the team decided to increase the brightness on our standard product from 89 to at least 92 and for our top of the line sheet, we were driven, at John Becker's insistence, to get one point better than our competitor—or a 96 bright—and the shade had to be "The perfect blue." I called the project: "The Search for the Perfect Blue."

Our brightness enhancement team was selected from a very diverse, cross-functional group. We had people on this team with educational backgrounds varying from high school to doctorate degrees. Positions ranged from marketing to machine crews to Mead Central Research's scientists. For this project, and for the first time in my experience here, we also used the expertise of one of our leading chemical suppliers. With research's guidance, Stuart Johns' Technical Services and Dave Wynn and Bill Fasoli-two of our paper machine superintendents-brought in several key chemical suppliers who all made presentations to the team. We then selected the supplier that seemed to have the greatest expertise in and knowledge of what we wanted to accomplish.

Part of what we learned from our suppliers was how optical brighteners and dyes really work and interact with each other. We learned that we had been wasting a lot of expensive materials that actually interfered with each other. During the developmental machine trials, we discovered some new application techniques that, to our knowledge, had not been utilized in the industry before. Our process is radically different, unique, and much simpler than before. We are more cost effective and have developed some new applications that we believe to be totally unique in the industry. We actually developed an entirely new range of products superior to any that our competitors have . . . *yet.* I'm glad we set our sights higher than we thought we could go.

While running the trials, we had Yuping Luo and Gurudas Khambadkone, two research technicians, covering the process around the clock. Stuart Johns from Tech Service and two technicians from the chemical supplier also were monitoring everything we were doing. Yuping and the supplier technicians would direct Stuart as to what to do and he was the designated "point man" between the technicians and the operators. We began the actual trials on the night shift to stabilize the machine so that it was ready to go at first light. I'd like to say it went off without a hitch, but that would be a bit untrue. We got to find out how a good team works when something goes wrong.

We gave the new specifications to our Quality Control team and the "color man," who is the person responsible for achieving the proper shade and matching the instrumental numbers that we wanted to achieve on our Colorimeter. We knew that the target numbers would produce a shade that was much bluer than we had ever run before and also much brighter. The first two reels we made looked like

"Smurf" paper. They were very blue. We found out that the pump we were using was putting too much dye into the system. We had to back off so the dye would just drip in. This is a system that is producing tons of paper and these few drops of dye were too much for the pump ... pretty concentrated stuff. So we jury-rigged a pump and about midway through the morning we actually started to make very bright paper. Unfortunately, we were still not hitting the Colorimeter specs for exact shade match.

A few minutes before noon, the brightness dropped out and we suddenly found ourselves back to the old pink shade of the eight-year old grade that we were trying to get away from. This was a disaster. It was brought to everyone's attention when Yuping, the very talented research scientist who did all of the pilot machine research on this project, came tearing down the hall by the superintendents' offices, yelling and screaming, obviously extremely upset to the point where we couldn't understand her. Hoping that someone had not gone through the paper machine, I asked, "What's wrong? What's going on?" She replied, "The color man changed back to the old formula; the trial is ruined."

It seems that the color man was so afraid he was making "broke" (which is off-spec paper that can't be sold) that he went off the trial run and "dropped back down in the dots" as we call it ... back to the security of the old technology which he knew and was comfortable with and which could be "sold." Our color people are very concerned about how much off-standard paper they allow to be produced because that is their individual responsibility. Our Quality Control team member, Jim Davis, saw the problem coming and was quick to point out (with his usual candor) the communication gap between the color technician and the rest of us. This really allowed us time to make the necessary corrective moves before getting into serious difficulty.

It seems we hadn't communicated to all the key

people in this instance. I had to call a timeout and get everybody into the machine lab for an emergency meeting. When all were assembled, I said, "Look, what I guess I didn't make clear was that our partner in this, our large greeting card company, has purchased every bit of this paper. They said they would use it all, except for the two 'Smurf-blue' reels." I continued, "This is someplace you've never been before, but the beauty of it is, everything you've run we've sold. And anything you have to throw away, I'm going to sign my name to—so you're off the hook"

We asked the color man if he could get back up out of the "dots" and try this new process, now that he understood he was not wasting the company's money. He became an entirely different part of the process after that and accomplished better results than we could have imagined. Yuping recovered without tranquilizers.

By 3:00 p.m. we had produced a reel of paper with 99 brightness. Finally, the whole run settled down and ran at about 98 which is, to my knowledge, the brightest sheet ever produced by an integrated mill like ours. This was truly a momentous occasion.

Our grades went up 4 brightness points on both the standard product and on the premium product. We created a win-win situation all the way around. This higher brightness product was cheaper to produce and was of greater value to our customer. Not only are our customers in the United States excited about this product, but our partners in the United Kingdom, Austria, and Germany are enamored with it as well. Mead now has a sheet equal to Europe's high-bright sheets. This is our mills' first "World Class" product!

We have a product here that is truly remarkable. We have a Chevrolet-priced product with the quality of a Cadillac. The change in chemistry in this product will save us over one-half million dollars a year and, with the enriched customer mix we will get from this product, we can expect to generate a lot more profit.

Skeptics, did you note that last paragraph? A "Chevrolet-priced product with the quality of a Cadillac." A savings of more than a half-million dollars a year, the expectation of a much larger customer base, and with it increased profits. That's what Creative Problem Solving can do for your bottom line.

After such a report, if you still don't think it's worth it, then I have but one last thought for you:

You had better hope your competitor thinks the same thing.

Evaluate Ideas Positively

———⊏⊐┼◈┼⊏⊐———

Acknowledge the negative, but accentuate the positive.
Telling people what they are doing wrong,
while ignoring what they are doing right,
reduces their energy.
GEORGE LEONARD,
author of *Mastery, Education and Ecstasy,* and *The Ultimate Athlete*

In my seminars I ask participants for their comments on a picture of an odd-looking wheelbarrow with a very large hopper, a short handle, and a wheel behind the hopper.

NEW WHEELBARROW DESIGN

Participants are asked to comment on the wheelbarrow design. Some comments I've received:
* ✷ "The hopper is too big."
* ✷ "The handle is too short."
* ✷ "The wheel is in the wrong place."
* ✷ "It will be hard to lift."
* ✷ "Go back to the drawing board, Roger"

You'll notice that all these "comments" are criticisms.

In real life, this wheelbarrow is used for high-rise construction. It is pulled up the side of a building on a crane. The construction worker pushes down on the handle instead of pulling up on it. By pushing down on the handle, the wheelbarrow has a lower center of gravity and is easier to control. That's very important if you are thirty-eight stories above the ground with only a safety net below. The wheelbarrow is used to haul items like the big rivets that construction workers use to hold buildings together.

I get some pretty pointed comments after I explain the contraption, such as: "You set us up! You didn't give us all the information on it. You didn't tell us what the wheelbarrow was to be used for."

Maybe so, but isn't that what most new ideas look like when they are first proposed? They look a little strange and a little odd, don't they? Often you don't have all the information about the new idea when you first see it.

A very powerful process goes on during my wheelbarrow exercise. What would happen if I took such comments and redrew or modified my wheelbarrow according to those comments? What would I have?

That's right. I would have the same old wheelbarrow. Without positively evaluating the "new" design, there would have been no innovation, no new ideas, no new market and no new sales. Most of the time, I find that the knee-jerk reaction to a new idea is to kill it.

So much for the odd wheelbarrow. Now let's get a bit more personal. How do *you* feel when people are asked to comment on a new idea you've developed, and all they do is criticize it?

You see, generating ideas to solve a problem is only part of the process; the next step is evaluating and building those ideas for action. How you evaluate those ideas is critical. It is crucial to evaluate the ideas of other people, coworkers, subordinates, and children without slaughtering their efforts and destroying their creativity or confidence in the process.

WHAT DIFFERENCE DOES IT MAKE?

A powerful example of a different approach to judging ideas appeared in a recent issue of *Possibilities* magazine.[1] Arthur Gordon wrote about the experiences of a friend who belonged to a club at the University of Wisconsin. Group members were a collection of brilliant boys; some possessed real literary talent. At each meeting, one would read a story or essay he had written and submit it to the criticism of the others.

Each manuscript was mercilessly dissected; no one pulled any punches. The critiques were so brutal that the club members dubbed themselves "The Stranglers."

Meanwhile, some women on campus formed a comparable group called "The Wranglers." The Wranglers also read their manuscripts aloud. Their criticism, however, fell more gently. The Wranglers hunted for kind things to say. All literary efforts, however feeble, were encouraged.

According to Gordon, the payoff came about twenty years later. Of the bright, young talent in the Stranglers, not one had made a literary reputation of any kind. Out of the Wranglers emerged a half-dozen successful writers, some of national prominence, led by Marjorie Kennan Rawlings who wrote "The Yearling."

Consider the environment for creativity in each of these situations. The amount of raw talent in the two groups was similar. But the Wranglers actively supported each other, while the Stranglers promoted self-criticism, self-disparagement, and self-doubt.

Sadly, my experience in business suggests that most organizations more closely follow the Stranglers' pattern than the Wranglers'. The question is, why? Why do we naturally gravitate toward the negative? I think the primary reason may be that we haven't been taught to look first at the strengths of an idea.

GUIDELINES FOR HANDLING IDEAS

Just as it is important to follow some specific guidelines for generating ideas, it is also crucial to use guidelines for *converging* on ideas. In *Creative Approaches to Problem Solving,* authors Scott Isaksen, Brian Dorval, and Don

Treffinger recommend the following guidelines for selecting ideas:[2]

1. *Use affirmative judgment.* Look for the strengths or positive aspects of an idea first. Only then should you focus on the concerns. Most ideas aren't born perfect and usually need some refining. Phrase your concerns about an idea in the form of a problem statement to encourage further development of the idea instead of disregarding it outright.
2. *Be deliberate.* Use a specific strategy for converging on ideas. Let the members of your team know your plan for making decisions. Keep your plan out in the open and don't select ideas based on some hidden agenda.
3. Don't overlook ideas that challenge your current assumptions or that are new or intriguing. Often these renegade thoughts can lead to new breakthroughs and innovative solutions to problems.
4. *Stay on course.* Sometimes the excitement generated in a fast-moving idea-generating session can lead you to lose sight of your original purpose. As you select ideas, keep your focus on the problem you want to solve.

No idea is perfect, but the way you deal with the imperfections of an idea makes the difference between an environment that is conducive to and one that is destructive to creativity.

PLUSES, POTENTIALS, AND CONCERNS
A wonderful tool exists to help you build on the strengths of an idea and give your coworkers the power to overcome any concerns they may have about it. The technique is called Pluses, Potentials, and Concerns (PPC).[3] PPC is designed to provide a structure for critically evaluating ideas in such a way that both the idea and the person proposing the idea are built up.
One of the most powerful changes you can make in

your behavior is to evaluative ideas using a balance of praise and criticism. In other words, positively evaluate ideas and then phrase your concerns about the idea in a way that the concerns can be overcome or refined, instead of destroying the idea with criticism. That is the purpose of the Pluses, Potentials, and Concerns technique.

Essentially, the technique works like this: When someone proposes an idea, stop your natural urge to destroy it. Take a moment to look carefully at the pluses, potentials, and concerns about the idea. When you discuss concerns, phrase them in the form of a problem statement or question.

Before anyone says this would take too much time or be too difficult to pull off, let me tell you a bit about where this technique originated and about the bottom line benefits of using a technique such as PPC.

A BRIEF HISTORY OF PPC

In the late 1960s a creativity consulting firm on the East Coast was conducting creativity seminars for businesses and industries. Seminar attendees came up with some pretty wild and unique concepts, many of which were also quite useful. Participants then evaluated the ideas and took the workable ones home to solve company problems.

When seminar participants began the evaluation process, they followed their usual routine: They focused on all the things that were wrong with the idea. As people left these creativity sessions, seminar leaders heard laments like, "You know, we had the beginning of some pretty powerful ideas in this session. But by the time we got done evaluating the ideas, all we had left were the same worn-out, old concepts."

At one seminar, several people from the same company noticed the idea slaughtering. They approached the two consultants who were conducting the session and suggested they speak with their company president who, as these participants explained it, had a unique way of dealing with ideas. The company was growing, doing well financially, had excellent relationships with customers and suppliers, and was a great place to work.

The consultants were intrigued and scheduled a meeting with the corporate president. A thirty-minute interview soon turned into a two hour meeting and lunch. The president wondered what they might find and was flattered that his employees noticed he was doing something right.

SCHEDULE YOUR TIME WELL

An effective Creative Problem Solving session has an agenda and a purpose. If you begin a session as the facilitator, welcome all the participants. Assure them that all of their contributions are important and necessary. Review the ground rules for generating ideas (chapters 5 and 6). Survey the Creative Problem Solving roles (chapter 6) and conduct a practice session to warm up the group. Introduce the client's problem and begin working. As a facilitator, regularly check with the client throughout the session to see if the options the group is generating are on track. If necessary the client can, without criticizing ideas, redirect the group.

In the first several meetings you should plan on spending about two to three hours. This time will allow you to train the group and make progress on your client's challenge. As you facilitate more meetings, you will be able to reduce the time it takes to effectively apply Creative Problem Solving, and you can make more educated choices regarding what aspect of the process will be most effective.

He told the consultants he really didn't know what he did, but he certainly wanted to find out so he could intentionally do it again and again. He allowed the consultants to shadow him for a week, sitting in on meetings and strategic conversations and walking through the plant with the president.

The consultants discovered the president evaluated ideas using a pluses, potentials, and concerns format. When someone approached him with a new idea, he became very conscious of what was about to occur: Someone in his company was about to give him an idea they thought could improve the organization, smooth out the work flow, reduce cycle time, or make more money. He became all ears, because he knew ideas helped his business improve. Ideas did not bother him; he saw them as opportunities.

When someone proposed an idea, the president would first mention several *pluses* (strengths, advantages, or good points of the idea). He would then discuss the *potentials* (spin-offs, opportunities, or possible future gains if the idea were to be implemented). Finally, he would address *concerns* posed by the idea. But instead of saying that the idea would cost too much, he would challenge the idea by asking, "How might you reduce the cost?" or "How might you raise the money to develop the idea?" Instead of saying, "Management will never accept this idea," he would rephrase his concern and ask, "How might you get management's support?"

Do you see how such an approach can revolutionize an organization's approach to new ideas? Just for a moment, put yourself in the place of the person who proposes an idea to that president. How would you feel if your idea were evaluated by discussing the pluses, potentials, and concerns of your idea, phrasing the latter in the form of a question? Would you be challenged, excited, ready to experiment with the idea? Would you go out and work hard to overcome the concerns and develop a fine-tuned concept?

Absolutely! That's exactly how the people in this company responded. When the consultants incorporated this approach into their training program, they found that participants worked to refine and develop some of the uniquely valuable ideas that otherwise would have been destroyed.

It's just possible some of you may be tempted to respond, "Well, that's nice, but I have to critically evaluate my people's ideas. We can't waste valuable time and money on dead ends." Unfortunately, most of us tend to confuse critical thinking with criticism. They are not the same.

Critical thinking is carefully examining an idea to look at both its strengths and weaknesses, not merely its shortcomings. When it is done right, it is worth far more than the time spent on it.

MORE POWERFUL THAN A SPEEDING CRITIC
Remember David Newcomer, head of Mead Fine Papers' Papeterie Marketing group? In the last chapter he described how his group applied Creative Problem Solving to enhance the brightness and shade of its greeting card papers, thus creating a competitive edge in the marketplace. Use of PPC was central to that effort. David says,

> One of the things that occurred as a result of training in Creative Problem Solving is that our upper management is now more open to new ideas than in the past. We're not a company that's invented a whole lot of new products lately, and caution had been the watchword in handling new ideas. We are now more open to empowering people to take creative approaches and some risk to develop new products or challenges.
> When we returned from your workshop, we put together a different team than we'd had in the past. We utilized your video-tape in our team training sessions and learned to use the PPC technique to evaluate ideas. We also laid the ground rules for generating ideas. This immediately started what I would consider dramatic personnel breakthroughs in our meetings held every other Friday.
> We have some rules to follow in these meetings. Up front, I insist that we will use no hard negatives in team meetings. We voice anything that would be considered potentially negative as a concern. In the beginning, we used the actual PPC forms from your workshop. After a while, people don't need the forms. Now the PPC method is pretty much ingrained and is the way we do business in these meetings. As a result of this, I think we were able to come up with a whole new manufacturing process that is truly an industry breakthrough.

When done right, PPC can be the very thing that helps your company obtain and use the creative edge it needs to succeed. But how do you access all the ideas that a Creative Problem Solving session generates? Again, Mead is a good example. It uses a software program to store and circulate these ideas throughout the organization.

According to Dave Newcomer, whenever Mead pulls a team together to generate ideas to solve a problem—whether it relates to marketing, technical, or paper making—all the resulting ideas are entered into the software program administered by Mead Central Research in Dayton, Ohio.

"We put in the ideas regardless of how ridiculous or wild they may appear," Dave says. After the input sessions,

> We sit down and pull up one by one the ideas that weren't screened in the initial creativity session. We estimate what it's going to cost to develop them. We try to determine the chances of success and what the payoff might be if the concept is successful. This is where we really address all the pluses, potentials, and concerns about an idea.
>
> We then take the ideas that have the highest priority and review them again. Some of the ideas might still be worth doing, but they are going to take a lot more time. We put those ideas on a different burner with different people working on them, but you keep them in the process. If the idea doesn't look like the payback is there, you put that in a different slot. But the beauty of this program is that you've captured the thought. You have it in the system and it is now available to the whole corporation. We have ideas in there from packaging, specialty papers, fine papers, and carbonless papers. Anyone can enter ideas into the system. In fact, I think we are at the point where we need to expand the availability of the idea base to even more divisions throughout the Mead organization.

And the dollar payoff? Dave says that while it is hard

to estimate, it's not hard to see. "Our carbonless paper division makes a type of paper that is experiencing a rapidly diminishing market," he says. "By creating or developing new products in that division, you are saving not only millions of dollars and increasing your mix, but you are also saving a lot of jobs and possibly creating more jobs in the process. The sessions in Chillicothe, Ohio, yielded well over 1,000 ideas and enhanced the creativity process. With the positive attitudes and the tools we have today, success is only a matter of time."

NOT EASY, BUT WELL WORTH IT

People across the country have told me that PPC is one of the most powerful and useful methods they have found for evaluating ideas, making decisions, and taking effective action. Pluses, Potentials, and Concerns organizes your thinking and helps you to overcome the concerns before they come back to haunt you.

Yet evaluating ideas with a Pluses, Potentials, and Concerns approach takes conscious effort—even for me, Mr. Creativity guy. When someone proposes an idea that really challenges the way I look at my business or life, I have to strongly resist the temptation to tear down the idea. We just have not been taught to think this way. I know I have the strategies to build on the idea—after all, I teach this stuff—but when an idea appears that (at first glance) I don't like, I sometimes slip and attack it. Then I must backtrack and work through the strengths of the idea. It's certainly true that following through on the strategy of PPC is not always easy, but I guarantee it's always worth the effort.

Several years ago I was invited to conduct one of my creativity programs with the toy design group at Fisher-Price. I was excited to work with the group—as well as very intimidated. What could I tell these people about creativity? After all, their daily job is to be creative. They design *toys.*

Before we began, some members of the group wanted to meet and talk informally with me. They asked me to join them for dinner the evening before our session. Now, if

I felt a little intimidated before dinner, I felt a whole lot more intimidated after we ate. The group was amazing. Members were not only bright and creative, but also vocal, articulate, and a little on the wild side. They were the epitome of what one might expect from highly creative toy designers.

I didn't sleep well that night. In fact, I thought about slinking away under cover of darkness, never to return. But I couldn't do that. I had a reputation to protect . . . at least I did before delivering the next day's program. When morning came and we began the session, they were ready for me. Generating ideas for these folks was a piece of cake. They could generate more ideas than any group I have ever worked with. It was nothing new for them.

Yet we did enjoy a breakthrough. It came when I taught members how to converge, focus, build, and positively evaluate ideas. They loved the PPC technique; in fact, they began using it within a few hours of my presentation.

That afternoon, group members presented new toy design ideas for two years in the future. The vice president of the division told me that this session usually ended up in a "blood bath." Designers would present their designs and these very creative people would immediately pounce on all the flaws. The ideas that survived either had to be extraordinarily well-developed with an immediate need in mind, or presented with great force.

That afternoon, it was different. Group members used the PPC approach to present their toy ideas and to evaluate them. I was told it was the most well-run, efficient, productive session ever held at Fisher-Price's annual toy design conference. People left the session with positive input that refined and strengthened their designs, as opposed to the traditional approach of total carnage.

All kinds of organizations can benefit from using PPC. St. John's United Church of Christ in Greeley, Colorado, uses PPC in its church council meetings to evaluate proposed ideas and courses of action. According to St. John's minister, Bill Royster, "the PPC technique gives us a focus to stay positive and productive about our ideas.

We wanted to be supportive of each other's ideas in our meetings, but we also wanted to be legitimate. Pluses, Potentials, and Concerns gives us a method to strengthen our ideas and build our proposed plans of action."

TRUST THE PROCESS

A word of caution: Don't try to short-circuit this process before you try it! Do the PPC technique as it is explained, *in order*. Do the pluses first, then the potentials, and last the concerns. Do not jump to concerns first simply because they come to your mind before the others. That's the way you typically evaluated ideas in the past—and, I might add, not too successfully.

Keep in mind that the first time you evaluate someone's idea using the PPC technique, the process will seem a bit uncomfortable and contrived. You will have to pay close attention to what you are doing. It might also feel a little awkward. Yet that's the way it is anytime you try something new. Remember the first time you tried to ride a bike or shoot a basket? Just remember, it becomes much easier with practice.

Put it firmly in mind that the PPC technique is designed to help you become conscious of the idea evaluation process so you can build the idea and encourage the person who is proposing it. It is also designed to help you strengthen your own ideas and build them for implementation. The PPC technique helps you to bring possibilities to reality.

So practice it; it works!

EIGHT

The Power of the PPC
—=□+◊+□—

*The normal reaction of most of us to a new idea
is either to ignore it, or instantly seek its defects.*
JOHN WILLIAMS

*Management that is destructively critical
when mistakes are made kills initiative.*
WILLIAM L. MCKNIGHT

The crucial thing to keep in mind about developing ideas
and planning for action is that refining ideas must be based
on the principle of *affirmative judgment*. When we practice
affirmative judgment, we consciously look to find the
strengths in an idea. This contrasts with the all-too-common
approach, which is immediately and energetically to point
out all the possible flaws of the new idea.

The whole purpose of the Pluses, Potentials, and
Concerns technique is to harness and direct a group's affirmative judgment. To apply the PPC technique, you, the
problem solver, need an idea or concept that you want to
develop. At this stage it is *not* necessary to have a clear path
or strategy of how to implement the idea.

This is important to recognize because most people
who have not been trained to develop ideas will often disre-
gard an idea that lacks a clear focus for action, and instead
will tend to return to some old, worn-out concept that they
know will work (however marginally). The PPC technique is
designed to help refine a promising idea to the point where
it can be effectively implemented.

ONE STEP AT A TIME
There are several steps in applying the PPC technique. Each
one should be taken in order; no substitutions, please!

**1. State the idea you want to develop in the form
of an idea phrase.**

The language we use to describe an idea is crucial. It tells our brain how to think about the idea. Begin your solution with the phrase, "What I see myself (us) doing is. . . ." When you use this phrase, it instructs your mind to start imagining what it will be like when you implement the solution. It tells your mind to picture what the concept might look like in action.

THE RIGHT WAY TO SAY NO

Leaders must walk a thin line. They must have a clear direction set for where the organization is going; they must listen to others' ideas; they must help their people work as a team; and they also need to say "no" sometimes. But when they say no, it needs to be said in a way that makes sense. People must understand the reason for the no; then they will come back with other ideas that could help the organization grow.

Your idea phrase should be written with a specific, measurable result in mind. The result can be as detailed as hours or dollars saved, a decrease in product defects, or measurable higher productivity, or as simple as verifying that you have accomplished your objective or not accomplished it.

A specific, measurable result is important because many people select ideas that are far too broad and general. These ideas are so broad that there would be no way to measure them even if it were possible to implement them. For example, in the latter part of my creativity seminars I ask people to list all of the key learnings they have acquired as a result of participating in the program. After they list their key learnings, I ask them to generate ideas for solving the problem of: "How might we use what we have learned about creativity in our personal or professional lives?" After they have generated a list of ideas for how they might apply their learnings, I ask them to select one on which to practice the PPC technique. This is the stage where people sometimes have trouble.

For example, one idea some participants have selected is "communication." Now, let's look at the idea of "communication." What does that mean? Verbal communication, non-verbal communication, sign language, smoke signals, reading books, writing books, producing a radio show, giving speeches? As you see, there is no specific, measurable result in the idea of "communication" The concept is much too broad.

To create a specific, measurable result from "communication" you might come up with ideas like:

✶ Publish a monthly newsletter
✶ Have the general manager produce a weekly video-tape that is given to all company employees
✶ Post information on every bulletin board in the building

Do you see the difference between the last three ideas and the idea of "communication"? The last three will result in a specific, measurable result, but "communication" is so broad a concept that there is no way to implement it.

2. List at least three good things about the idea. These three traits are the pluses of the idea. They are the strengths or positive aspects of the concept. This is what's good about the idea, at face value, right now.

3. List the potentials. Potentials are spinoffs, speculations, or possible future gains that might result if the idea were implemented. These are the results it might create. Of course, potentials can be either positive or negative. But if the potentials point out a major concern that may prevent the idea from being implemented, or produce grave circumstances in the organization, they should be dealt with as concerns.

4. List the concerns about the idea. Concerns must be worded as problem statements if this technique is to work. Problem statements begin with the words, "How to ..." or "How might I . . ." When the concerns are phrased like a problem statement, your mind recognizes them as something that can be solved and almost immediately begins to generate ideas. The concerns must be phrased like a problem statement if you are going to make any progress on developing the idea.

For example, if the concern is that the idea will cost too much, rephrase your concern as "How to reduce the cost?" or "How to find the money to develop the idea?" By phrasing concerns in this way, you can generate ideas to overcome the concern, strengthen the concept, and increase its chances for acceptance. This is a positive, proactive approach to evaluating and building ideas.

5. *Overcome your concerns about the idea.* After you have listed your concerns, generate ways to overcome each of the them. Decide which one should be overcome first. Sometimes when people tackle their toughest concern first, one or even two of their other concerns evaporate. The included form (pages 128-133) has space for three concerns, but you can certainly deal with more.

Over the course of my career, I have found it interesting that the average number of concerns is about three, even with tough organizational problems. When you think about where the PPC technique occurs in the creative process, you have already defined a good problem statement, generated ideas, and then picked the best idea available from your list of many.

After you have generated enough ideas to overcome the concerns, review those ideas and develop an improved statement of the solution. Phrase this improved statement of the solution using the words, "What I *now* see myself doing is. . .

6. *Develop action steps to implement the solution.* After you create your improved statement of the solution, then use the questions on the Pluses, Potentials, Concerns, and Planning for Action form at the end of this chapter. These questions are designed to prompt your thinking to generate action steps to help you implement your solution. They are designed to help polish out any rough spots that might still exist in your solution.

7. *Review your action steps and develop a plan.* Decide what is going to be done, who will do it, by when, and who will check to be sure it is done. Divide the action steps into short-term, intermediate, and longer term action steps. You can establish your own time frame for short-term, intermediate, or long-term action. (Short-term for a sales person might be in the next three days, while short-term for a research scientist might be a year.)

Together these steps will create a step-by-step plan for action. It is important in the development of such a plan to identify one short-term action that can be accomplished within twenty-four hours after the session concludes, even if this action step is merely to look up a phone number in the telephone book. Momentum is essential in the creative process; an action, even a small one, is crucial in creating the required momentum for change.

TO PROPOSE IDEAS UP THE LADDER

If you need to propose ideas "up the ladder" in your organization (and you are afraid you are going to be shot down by all sorts of reasons why your new solution won't work), then take the idea development into your own hands and develop it before it ever gets to your boss. You might try the following approach to proposing an idea when you have your discussion with your boss:

> Here is an idea we have been working on. Here are the pluses or strengths of the idea; here are the potentials of the idea; and oh yes, here are all the concerns we know you might have about the idea. We have developed about twenty ways to overcome each of these concerns and a step-by-step plan for action. When would you like to start?

Contrast this with the usual approach of unfocused discussions or sessions where the idea gets so shot full of objections that it will never be implemented. Anticipate objections and have at least twenty ideas ready to overcome them. Develop a plan for implementing the idea so that your boss doesn't have to try to figure out how to get the idea into the organization.

Also, consider your boss's possible reaction when you propose the idea. Remember the reaction of my seminar participants when I showed them the crazy-looking wheelbarrow! Your idea might look like a wheelbarrow to your boss. Had my seminar participants possessed some more information on the wheelbarrow idea, had they known some of the pluses, potentials, and concerns about the idea, had they some idea of what the wheelbarrow might be used for, no doubt they would have reacted very differently to the design. So give your idea a chance for a fair hearing by using PPC to raise the "threshold of acceptability" so your idea can be implemented.

ENLISTING THE SUPPORT OF OTHERS

Once you have evaluated your idea, overcome your concerns, and developed ideas for action, how are you going to enlist the support of others to help you implement your solution and make a difference in your organization? What can you do when you need to explicitly and systematically show the value of your idea to other people in your organization?

Everett M. Rogers is an expert on the diffusion of innovations. He has researched how people adopt new products, services, or lifestyle practices. Rogers has investigated the diffusion of such innovations as the adoption of birth control in Third World countries to the infusion of personal computers across America.

His research has isolated five qualities of innovations that help to speed their acceptance and subsequent adoption.[1] Those attributes are:

1. Relative advantage
2. Compatibility
3. Complexity
4. Trial ability
5. Observability

Relative Advantage is a measure of how much better an innovation is than the idea or product it replaces. This is one of the most common and most effective approaches to selling an idea. It is important to keep in mind, however, that your idea must clearly illustrate its advantages in terms of low cost, decrease in discomfort, or savings in time and effort.

continued on page 123

continued from page 122

Compatibility asks, "Is your idea consistent with the values, past experiences and needs of those individuals or groups who will potentially adopt it?" It is highly unlikely that you will purchase a product or change aspects of your lifestyle that oppose your values. It is much more likely that you will adopt innovations that support them.

Recycling is an excellent example of compatibility. Many more people recycle their refuse or purchase environmentally safe products than in the past because these products are compatible with our current values of conserving our planet.

Complexity gauges how difficult it is to understand or use an innovation. Be careful with this one! The more complex your idea appears to be, the less likely it will be accepted. Keep it simple. Probably one of the best examples of how keeping it simple led to a successful product launch is the Macintosh computer. Remember when you were terrified of using a computer because it was so complicated? Macintosh's main selling point was "If you can point, you can use this computer." Millions of dollars in sales later, the competition finally caught on.

Trial ability allows potential adopters or customers to experiment with the idea before "buying it." Test driving a new car is an excellent example of trial ability. If your idea is not something that can be "test driven," it is important to find a way to allow your customers to experiment with it on a limited basis. The question to keep in mind here is: "How can my potential adopters try before they buy?"

Finally, *observability* refers to some aspect of your innovation that people can see. If you are selling an intangible idea or concept (such as life insurance), what is the visible result of what you are buying? In what ways can you make the results tangible? Can people actually see the results? How about a model? Can you take your potential customers to other locations that have adopted the idea so they can see it in action? Remember this one: Seeing is believing.

continued on page 124

continued from page 123
Whether you are a mayor, a corporate president, a salesperson, or a parent, the next time you are trying to convince someone of the value of your idea, product, or service, take some time to examine it systematically in light of Rogers' research. Use the five diffusion qualities as a checklist to improve, refine, and empower your strategy to increase the chances that others will support and adopt your idea.

IF PEOPLE PROPOSE IDEAS TO YOU

If you are the boss to whom people must come to get their ideas implemented—and if you are afraid that you are having "wheelbarrow" reactions—then train your people to try the PPC technique on their ideas before they bring them to you. Have them work through the PPC form and smooth out the rough spots so you can see how the idea might be implemented and the value it could add to your organization.

CREATIVE PROBLEM SOLVING IN THE CHURCH

The PPC technique and the rest of the elements of Creative Problem Solving can be applied to any organization, business, or group, even in the church! Let me end this chapter with a couple of stories.

St. John's United Church of Christ in Greeley, Colorado, is my home church. Recently the pastor of St. John's, Bill Royster, asked me to do a series of workshops for the northern Colorado business community, for members of St. John's, and for the Northeast Association of the Rocky Mountain Conference of the United Church of Christ. Bill had this to say on the use of Creative Problem Solving in the church, used with his permission:

> Around forty people from St. John's attended your workshop in January. Most of our church consistory, which is the official board of the church, were present as well as the majority of church committee leadership. They took this stuff seriously. At the very first consistory meeting after your session, Jim Parker

(the president of the consistory) and I reviewed the Pluses, Potentials, and Concerns (PPC) technique with the board members. Jim asked consistory members to use the PPC technique whenever we could, and especially when we needed to make some decisions. So, in a sense, the PPC technique was "lurking in the background" either as a threat or as a promise for any decisions we had to make.

This became most apparent at the September consistory meeting when Jim and I asked the board to consider a recommendation that a group doing alcohol and drug abuse therapy with eighty to one hundred teenagers be allowed to use the church every Tuesday night. This group had outgrown the space it was currently using and needed a larger place to meet. Now, Tuesday night also happens to be the night that the consistory meets, along with many church committees. So there was the possibility of battle lines being drawn. It could have been, "You mean we're supposed to give up our building for these drugged-out kids?"

When we presented the issue-that these kids needed a place to meet because they had outgrown the one they had—one person said, "Well, you know, that is the night that we use the building a lot." Then immediately someone else said, "But there is the potential here of providing a place for all these kids who have no other place to meet."

Now, no one said, "Well, let's do a PPC." But the very first word out of the second speaker's mouth was focused on the potential of the idea.

The next response was really interesting. The group actually began to overcome the concerns.

"You know, consistory could meet in private homes. Can we change our meeting?"

"Well, gosh, we can meet at my house."

This began a discussion of how we could make the idea work. Finally, there was one concern from a church trustee, one of the people who "guard" the building.

"With all these kids around, there's probably going to be a little damage," he said, "but we're not going to worry about it. We can take care of that."

The outcome: The consistory voted unanimously to turn the building over to this outside group that no one had ever seen or heard of before, except me. It's just amazing.

I must confess that, as an "insider," I was amazed. Growing up at St. John's was a conservative experience, to say the least. For the church consistory to allow the building to be used for free by a group of teenagers who had been involved with drugs–and who only the minister and the church board president had met–that's nothing short of remarkable.

Bill's comment regarding the PPC technique "lurking in the back-ground" surfaced again in another account about a group of retired men at St. John's (known as "the Doughnut Gang") who have applied creativity principles in their lives. Here is Bill's second story:

It occurred to me as I was thinking about PPC and the creative problem solving process that there is a small group of retired men known as the Doughnut Gang. The joke around the church is, feed these guys doughnuts and they'll do anything ... and they do! About four of the eight men in the doughnut gang were in that January workshop. The curious thing is that I don't believe these guys have said "No, it won't work" to anything, especially since your program. The joke for these guys is, "Well, let's see what Gail, my wife, thinks of next."

"So you want to hang stars up in the point of the ceiling thirty-eight feet above the floor for Christmas? Not a problem. We'll figure this one out."

Or, "You want us to build simulated organ pipes that we can mount on a wall so we can dedicate a new hymnal? Not a problem. We'll go to the carpet store. We'll get the big spools they wind carpet on. We'll cut them the right length, paint them black and just sort of tack them to the wall."

Creative Problem Solving permeates that retired group of guys. One could expect them normally to be in the retired, negative bunch. They drink coffee and eat doughnuts. I never hear them say, "Let's try PPC." But it's in the background constantly, lurking there, helping them focus on how to make things happen.

How effective is the PPC technique? Bill's two stories should give you an idea. But beyond what's happening in Greeley, by using the PPC technique alone, I have helped organizations develop sales plans, revise their management structures, and develop new product implementation strategies in a fraction of the time it would have taken without this approach. In one case, we were able to develop a new product strategy in three hours instead of the three weeks this organization normally took.

That, my friends, translates to real dollars. And we can all use a few more of those.

PLUSES, POTENTIALS, AND CONCERNS

If your ideas blend together or suggest a tentative plan of action, write your idea in the form of an idea phrase. Your idea phrase should be written with a specific, measurable result in mind. The result can be as detailed as using measures to quantify the result (metrics or dollars saved), or as simple as verifying that you have accomplished the solution or not accomplished it. Write your idea phrase below.

What I see myself (us) doing is:

Below list at least three *pluses* or specific strengths of your idea phrase. What is good about your idea now?

1.

2.

3.

Now, list three *potentials*, speculations, spinoffs, or possible future gains of your idea. What opportunities might result if your idea were implemented? List potentials beginning with the words: "It might."

1. It might:

2. It might:

3. It might:

Finally, list whatever *concerns* you have about your idea. Be sure to phrase concerns in the form of a problem statement so you can overcome each one of them. That sets the stage for you to develop a plan for action.

How to . . . ?

How to . . . ?

How to . . . ?

Now review the concerns you've just listed. Decide which concern is the most important one for you. List your most important concern below and generate at least fifteen ways to overcome that concern. After you believe you have enough ideas to overcome your most important concern, go to your next most important concern and generate ways to overcome that concern. Do this until all of your concerns have been overcome.

Concern 1 . How to . . . ?

Ideas for overcoming concern one:

1.

2.

3.

4.

5.

6.

7.

8.

9.

10.

11.

12.

13.

14.

15.

16.

17.

18.

Concern 2. How to . . .

Ideas for overcoming concern two:

1.	10.
2.	11.
3.	12.
4.	13.
5.	14.
6.	15.
7.	16.
8.	17.
9.	18.

Concern 3. How to ... ?

Ideas for overcoming concern three:

1.	10.
2.	11.
3.	12.
4.	13.
5.	14.
6.	15.
7.	16.
8.	17.
9.	18.

Now review the information that you wrote down for Pluses, Potentials, and Concerns, and especially the ideas you generated for overcoming your concerns. Write an improved statement of your solution below.

What I *now* see myself doing is:

Now generate at least twenty action steps that will detail everything that might need to happen to bring your solution to reality.

1.	11.
2.	12.
3.	13.
4.	14.
5.	15.
6.	16.
7.	17.
8.	18.
9.	19.
10.	20.

If you get stuck or begin to slow down, ask yourself the following questions to help you create more action steps:

* Who might assist you with your solution?
* Who do you need to convince about the merits of your solution?
* What steps might you take to put your solution into

action?
* What additional resources might help you to implement your idea (e.g., individuals, groups, materials, money)?
* What might you do to gain acceptance of your solution?
* What might you do to gain enthusiasm for your solution?
* What are some things that you might need to work to overcome?
* Where might you start?
* What special places or locations might you use?
* What are some places or locations to avoid?
* When might be a good time to begin?
* What special times might you use?
* How might you pretest your solution?

When you have generated all of the steps that need to be taken to bring your solution to reality, select the ones that you need to accomplish and then put them into the following format so that you know:

* What the specific action step is that will take place (be as specific as you can).
* Who is going to do this action step?
* By when will this action step be completed?
* Who will check to make sure it is done (to provide support; also, sometimes it helps to have someone check up on the person who will do the action step, just to make sure it isn't forgotten)?

Be sure to make one of your first steps something you can accomplish within the next twenty-four hours. Remember, momentum is essential in the creative process!

PLAN OF ACTION

What is going to be done?	Who will do it?	By when?	Who will check/ support?
Short-Term From_____ To_____			
Intermediate Term From_____ To_____			
Long-Term From_____ To_____			

Praise and Recognize Ideas

—⊐◈⊏—

No stimulus to creative effort is as effective
as a good pat on the back.
ERNEST BENGER

It is very difficult to produce new ideas in a situation where
the predominant attitude is one of criticism.
K. F. JACKSON

The world of education provides us with some fascinating information on the use of praise, criticism, and learning. Research has shown that it takes something like a four-to-one praise-to-criticism ratio just to keep students on track. Changing their behavior requires a significantly higher praise-to-criticism ratio-about eight-to-one.[1] In another study, researchers analyzed the way teachers *really* attempted to change student behaviors. What did they find? The *actual* praise-to-criticism ratio was exactly the opposite of what was needed-about one praise to four criticisms.[2]

I believe that good teachers are good leaders and that good leaders are good teachers. The question is, leader, how do you use praise in your organization? How do you use criticism? How do you use praise to help people put items on the agenda instead of using criticism to take things off? How do you use praise to support ideas and people, rather than using criticism to destroy them?

PRAISE, CRITICISM, AND CREATIVITY
Just what is the leader's role in praise and creative productivity? Recently I conducted a creativity training program for one of the world's largest chemical and consumer products manufacturing companies. In the audience was one of the firm's most creatively productive research and development scien-

tists. Soon after I presented the preceding statistics on praise and criticism, I looked over and noticed him smiling. During the break he came up to me and said,

> What you had to say about praise and criticism really hit home. You might have noticed that I was smiling at you after you mentioned that statistic. From 1978 to 1984 I had very negative bosses and I had the worst time of my life at work. I put together a list of my bosses since 1984. For ten years I had a string of bosses ranging from very good, to excellent, to "the best." They had nothing but praises and very few negative comments. I was receiving constant positive feedback by electronic mail or in person. Those praises propelled my creativity. I had my ten best years of creativity from 1984-1994. I had five bosses in the last ten years that I rated at 8, 8, 8, 9, 10 on a scale of 1-10, 10 being the best. I would say that these folks used maybe 100/1 ratio or even higher for praise to criticism. How wonderful it was! It was a terrific win-win situation for the employee and the company both.

Would you like "a terrific win-win situation for the employee and the company both" in your own organization? If so, then you need to spend some time analyzing your own praise-to-criticism habits. If the research scientist above were your employee, what kind of rating do you think he'd *give you?*

THE IMPORTANCE OF RECOGNITION
Studies and experience both show that encouragement and recognition play a major role in stimulating creativity and innovation in research and development organizations. It's no accident that the chemical research scientist above emphasized it. But what about in other organizations?

Peter Grazer, an international consultant who specializes in employee involvement and team development, had some interesting comments about recognition in a recent edition of *Employee Involvement Newsletter:*

In 1981 I was working as the project engineer on a construction project to modernize a silicon manufacturing facility in St. Louis, Missouri. We, as the project's management, had begun an employee involvement process (although we didn't call it that back then) to help the trades people improve performance.

About six months into the project, it came to our attention that a crew of ironworkers had completed the erection of some structural steel in one of the operating areas of the plant. Although the task was a difficult one, the ironworkers completed the work weeks ahead of schedule, well under budget, and without safety problems or other incidents. In short, it was an outstanding job.

Our newly formed "steering committee" talked about the effort and decided that somehow these people must be thanked for their contribution. We subsequently sent letters to their homes, thanking them for their outstanding work and inviting them and their wives to a dinner in their honor at a nice hotel in St. Louis.

The dinner was held on a Friday night and, to lighten the atmosphere, the manager "roasted" the crew members. It was an outstanding evening.

The following Monday morning I was walking around the site when I came upon one of the crew members. Jerry was in his fifties, usually loud and jovial, and naturally hardened from his years working with steel. But on this morning he was unusually quiet, appearing deep in thought.

Since we had just held the dinner the previous Friday, I asked Jerry if anything was wrong.

"You remember those letters you sent to our homes?" he asked. "When I arrived home that day my wife was waiting for me at the door—with the letter in her hands and tears in her eyes. And she said to me, `Jerry, you've been an ironworker for thirty years, and nobody's ever thanked you for anything. . . '"

Jerry paused, and we both stood there quietly for a moment. I thought, *How is it possible that someone could work for thirty years and not be thanked for anything he did?*

I didn't know at the time that this was the first of what would become more than 200 incidents like it during the next five years. Through these incidents I have come to believe that, in the work-place, we just don't thank people enough for their contributions. Recognition is woefully lacking.

The need for recognition, as one of our more sophisticated needs, is one of the most difficult to achieve. It is the only one on which we are wholly dependent upon others to respond appropriately. In other words, recognition, by definition, must come from others.

I wondered for years why so many recipients would experience any emotional response (such as tears) when receiving some recognition. What I came to understand was that they were finally breaking through a barrier (need fulfillment) that they had spent years striving for. Someone had finally thanked them for their good work.[3]

A BIG ERROR TO AVOID

One reason why some recent management innovations have failed is that they impose an external, often limiting structure on people. You cannot force creativity on your employees.

"It's 4:00 on Friday afternoon, we haven't had our creativity time yet this week, so everybody get creative now." Or, "You must do three brain-storming sessions a month, otherwise you haven't implemented our new creativity program."

Wrong!

Creativity is not something that comes from an external, mandated structure. It is something we all possess. You were born creative. Unfortunately, over the years we have learned some limiting behaviors that have blocked our ability to tap our natural creative resources.

Recognition and praise seem pretty simple, don't they? They are also inexpensive. They simply ask the leader to be aware that recognition and praise are crucial to establish not only the environment for creativity, but an environment for productivity as well.

CREATIVITY, PRAISE, AND YOUR BRAIN

I always thought I could control the effect that destructive criticism had on me. I believed that, even if I worked in a hostile environment that didn't exactly support my creativity, my brain could still come up with some reasonably good ideas. *By golly, I'll be creative in spite of all the criticism*, I'd think. After all, the criticisms were outside of me. Even if they upset me, I could choose to "let them in" or not.

I now believe that I was wrong.

Recently I was working on a project for a major international accounting firm. This firm is dramatically redesigning one of its divisions to create a learning organization, an organization in which people not only work hard, but create and learn to do their jobs better in quicker, more effective ways. This company was interested in making Creative Problem Solving a way of doing business and creating a learning environment in which its training would become much more effective. Management was also interested in reducing the cycle time necessary to redesign training to develop that competitive edge.

One of the collaborators on this project was Dave Meier, Director of the Center for Accelerated Learning in Lake Geneva, Wisconsin. Dave has helped organizations ranging from Alcoa to American Express, from M&M Mars to Chevron to NASA. Dave knows how to engineer success. For example, he has helped New York Telephone cut its failure rate from 40 percent to 2 percent in its customer service training; enabled Travelers Insurance to increase its success rate by 53 percent in teaching service representatives a new computer system for processing medical claims; and helped Commonwealth Edison, one of the largest public utilities in the United States, cut course training time in half while significantly increasing class evaluations and test scores.

In a session on learning, Dave presented a simplified model of the brain and its effect on learning. His work is based on the research of Dr. Paul McLean, who wrote the book *The Triune Brain*. Before we embark on a discussion of the brain and learning, please keep in mind that this is a very simplified explanation. The brain is a magnificent mystery that we can talk about only metaphorically and simplistically. Nevertheless, the discussion is useful. Essentially, the brain is made up of three parts. We have a brain stem, a limbic system, and a neo-cortex.

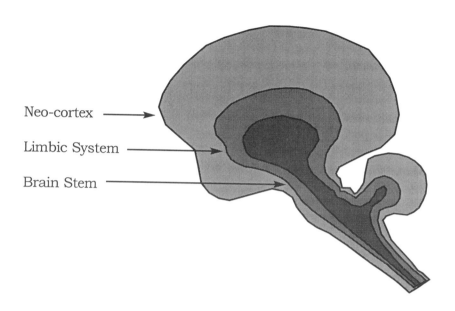

Neo-cortex

Limbic System

Brain Stem

The brain stem, in McLean's view, is the fundamental or basic part of the mind. It is also known as the reptilian brain. He believes it is the only evolutionary residue of the creatures which survived the aeons; the ones that didn't survive lacked a good reptilian brain. The most important intelligence is how to get food and how to keep from becoming food. The brain stem immediately tells its owner how to react when there's not much time to think.

The brain stem is common to many creatures, particularly mammals, and it is designed to sustain all physical survival. It is very instinctual (stimulus-response) and quick to make decisions. It is concerned with survival, either physical or psychological. It is also the part of the brain that has been analyzed the most by behaviorists.

Creatures with only a brain stem, like reptiles, won't rear their young. They don't know their young and they certainly won't be emotionally connected with the process of birth.

According to Dave Meier, the reptilian brain was the part most honored during the industrial age. People were placed on an assembly line and trained to do a specialized job over and over again. "Shovel coal, make steel, put a lug nut on a wheel. Repeat, repeat, repeat." In this organizational view, the worker does not think. All the thinking is done by management; workers are simply not intelligent enough to have any ideas.

Surrounding the brain stem is the limbic system, a chemical factory for producing hormones and other brain/body substances that affect our moods and bodily functions. It contains the equipment for processing emotions and governs how we feel about things. This part of the brain produces chemicals that can make us either sick or well. Creatures with a limbic system have feelings and also rear their young. If the brain stem can be represented by "repeat, repeat, repeat," then the limbic system can be represented by "feel, feel, feel."

Sitting on "top" of the limbic system is the neo-cortex or "new brain." This part of the brain controls the ability to speak, to think, to solve problems, and to learn. The neo-cortex is the learning brain, the thinking brain, the problem-solving brain. It is preeminent in the act of creation.

Although all three parts of the brain are interdependent, if you lose the frontal lobes of your neo-cortex, you can forget about being creative. (That is, if you could remember that you could forget.) If the brain stem says "repeat, repeat, repeat" and the limbic system says, "feel, feel, feel," then the neo-cortex says "create, create, create, and learn, learn, learn."

Such is the simplified triune brain theory.

So how does all this relate to your ability to foster creativity in the people who work with and for you? The connection comes in what Dave Meier calls "up shifting" and "down shifting."

Remember, this is a metaphorical look at what occurs in the brain. When you are in a physically or psychologically threatening situation, your feelings will be negative. As such, your limbic system will produce chemicals that depress the thinking part of your brain. You then move to the survival mode, "downshifting" into your reptilian function. Your predominant thoughts would be something like, *How can I survive this? What can I do to get through this?* You become reactive.

People in business can become "reptilian" in just this way. Dave Meier saw this happen when he worked with a major airline undergoing some very difficult times. The CEO (or someone just below the CEO) told his employees, "Hey, listen! You screw up and you're out of here." This occurred at a time when the company needed to be creative about its business, yet no one dared to put forward any new ideas. Why not? Because they were afraid. They were reacting instinctively with their reptilian brain.

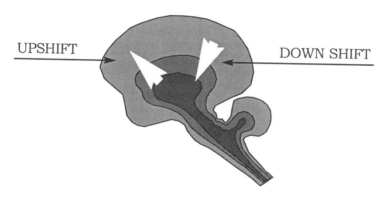

UPSHIFT · DOWN SHIFT

According to Robert Eckert, Senior partner in the consulting firm "New and Improved", your brain reacts neurochemically the same to the fear of being killed as it does to the fear of being rejected.[4] Talk about "down shifting!" People at the airline couldn't create because the environment was so punitive. People in this organization were so focused on survival (which forced them to react from their reptilian brains) that they couldn't begin to develop any new ideas. An organization or organism can't evolve if its main concern is survival.

"Up shifting," on the other hand, is the reverse. As Dave Meier is fond of saying, "When the soul is happy, your learning is snappy." Children, for example, are great learners when they are unconcerned about their immediate survival. In a sense, they are "out of themselves" and into their higher minds. They are thinking from their neo-cortex: Create, create,

create.

Meier believes we are naturally intended to be "up shift-ed" as much as possible. Downshifting is simply a protective device needed for survival. If we continually live in a defensive, downshifted state, however, we can become pathological.

That is why it is crucial in any learning situation-and hence any situation that involves creating new ideas-that you create a caring, protective, positive, even loving environment that allows people to be free to make mis-takes, to be the falli-ble creatures we all are, without fear of punitive action. Negative criticism causes us to downshift into the reptilian brain, while praise and recognition prompt us to upshift and use the full power of the neo-cortex. Then we are free to learn. Then we are free to create.
And then we are free to succeed.

EMOTIONAL INTELLIGENCE AND PRAISE
This is exactly the message that Daniel Goleman delivers in his intriguing book, *Emotional Intelligence.* He stressed that the connections between the limbic system and the neo-cortex are the "hub of the battles or cooperative treaties struck between head and heart, thought and feeling." This connection explains why emotion is crucial to effective thought, whether it is in making wise decisions, creating new ideas, or allowing us to think clearly.

Emotions can be powerful disrupters to clear thinking. Neuroscientists use the term "working memory" to describe the capacity of attention that holds in mind the data essential for completing a specific task or solving a problem-whether it be specific features you desire when house hunting or the ele-ments of a reasoning problem on a test.

The prefrontal cortex is the region of the brain that is responsible for working memory. But when circuits from the limbic system to the pre-frontal lobes signal strong emotion, like anxiety and anger, "neural static" can be created, which sabotages the ability of the prefrontal lobe to maintain working memory. This is the reason why, when we are emotionally upset, we say we "just can't think straight." This is also the reason why continual emotional distress can create deficits in a child's intellectual abilities, crippling the capacity to learn.

USE AN APPROPRIATE GROUP SIZE

An effective Creative Problem Solving resource group is five to seven people. If there are less than five people in a group, the members will be working pretty hard to generate problem statements and ideas. If you have more than seven people in a group, a behavior called "social loafing" often occurs. Social loafing happens when the group is big enough for members of the group to "hide" in it. In groups larger than seven people, it is much easier for one or two members to hang back and not participate. So, if you have more people involved in the problem, you might consider forming two sub-groups with a facilitator in each group.

It is also helpful to have a facilitator assistant who has equal or more experience. This "process buddy" can remind the facilitator of the appropriate CPS techniques to use, help to post flip chart paper and give the facilitator another pair of eyes and ears to monitor the group process.

Let me reiterate, whenever you conduct a Creative Problem Solving session, make sure you have a reason to do it. If the purpose of the session is to generate ideas, then make sure you have a well-defined problem statement as explained in chapters 3 and 4.

Emotions play a role in even the most "rational" decision making. Goleman, in *Emotional Intelligence*, cites the work of Dr. Antonia Damasio, a neurologist at the University of Iowa College of Medicine. Damasio has investigated what is impaired in patients with damage to the centers of the brain that control emotions. He found that their decision making becomes "terribly flawed"–and yet they show no deterioration at all in IQ or any cognitive ability. Even though their "intelligence" is intact, they can make disastrous choices in business and their personal lives. Their decisions are so bad because they have lost access to their *emotional* learning.

Feelings are crucial to help us make rational decisions. They direct us in the proper direction where simple logic can then be of best use. The world often confronts us with an unwieldy array of choices. (Where should you live? Whom should you marry? How should you invest your savings?) The emotional learning that we have received through life (such as the memory of a bad investment or a painful breakup) send signals that streamline the decision by eliminating some options and highlighting others. It is in this way, Dr. Damasio argues, "the emotional brain is as involved in reasoning as is the thinking brain."

The point is this: In our organizations we need to create an environment that's happy, an environment where people are positively reinforced and where they're feeling good about themselves. Praise and recognition have a powerful physiological effect on all of us. Environments that are punitive "downshift" us and encourage us to think poorly, while environments that are positive and uplifting—where there's a good superior/subordinate relationship, where the superior praises people and does not hold over them threats of punishment—"upshift" us and help to create a company primed for success.

The role of the leader is to praise the people he's working with, thus creating an environment that is positive and supportive. A good leader doesn't want to create an environment that is frenetic, negative, that puts people down. Through praise and recognition leaders should nudge people toward the agendas that they want to create, as opposed to forcing them through negative reinforcement.

CRITICISM DOESN'T WORK, ANYWAY

In any event, frequent negative criticism doesn't produce the results we want. In fact, it has exactly the opposite effect. When a leader withholds praise and recognition and instead doles out criticism and threats by the barrelful, his company suffers.

For example, a common form of destructive criticism in the workplace is a blanket, generalized statement like, "You are really screwing up," delivered in a sarcastic, harsh, angry tone, that does not provide a chance to respond or provide any suggestions on how to improve performance. This form of criticism leaves the person receiving it feeling helpless and angry. It shows an ignorance of the feelings it will trigger in those who receive the criticism and the devastating effect those feelings will have on their motivation, energy, confidence, and enthusiasm in doing their work.

Goleman reported on the results of a survey in which managers were asked to recall times they blew up at employees and, in the heat of the moment, made a personal attack: "The employees who received these attacks reacted most often by becoming defensive, making excuses, or evading responsibilities, or they stonewalled-that is, they tried to avoid all contact with the managers who blew up at them."

This was evidenced in a study reported by Goleman:

> Indeed, in a study of 108 managers and white collar workers, inept criticism was ahead of mistrust, personality struggles, and disputes over power and pay as a reason for conflict on the job. An experiment done at Rensselaer Polytechnic Institute shows just how damaging to working relationships a cutting criticism can be. In a simulation, volunteers were given the task of creating an ad for a new shampoo. Another volunteer (a confederate) supposedly judged the proposed ads: Volunteers actually received one of two prearranged criticisms. One critique was considered specific, but the other included threats and blamed the person's innate deficiencies with remarks like, "Didn't even try; can't seem to do anything right," and "Maybe it's just a lack of talent. I'll try to get someone else to do it.[5]

It certainly is understandable that those who were attacked became angry, tense, and antagonistic. Some said that they would not collaborate or cooperate on future projects with the person who gave the criticism. Many of the participants in the study indicated that they would want to avoid contact altogether. The harsh criticism made those who received it so demoralized that they no longer worked as hard and, in some cases, said they no longer felt capable of doing well. The personal attack was devastating to their morale.

Unfortunately, many managers are too willing to criticize, but stingy with praise. This leaves their employees feeling that they hear only about how they are doing when they make mistakes. This propensity to criticize is compounded by managers delaying giving any feedback at all for long periods.

"Most problems in an employee's performance are not sudden, they develop over time." J. R. Larson, a University of Illinois at Urbana psychologist, notes, "When the boss fails to let his feelings be known promptly, it leads to his frustration building up slowly. Then one day he blows up about it. If the criticism had been given earlier on, the employee would have been able to correct the problem?[6]

Too often people criticize only when things boil over or when they get too angry to control themselves. This is when they give criticism in the worst way, usually in a tone of biting sarcasm, listing grievances they have kept to themselves or making threats. These attacks backfire. They are received as an affront, so the recipient becomes angry in return. This is the worst way to motivate someone.

Consider the alternative:

> An artful critique can be one of the most helpful mes-
> sages a manager can send. . . An artful critique focuses
> on what a person has done and can do rather than
> reading a mark of character into a job poorly done. As
> Larson observes, "A character attack—calling someone
> stupid or incompetent—misses the point. You immedi-
> ately put him on the defensive, so that he no longer is
> receptive to what you have to tell him about how to do
> things better." . . In terms of motivation, when people
> believe that their failures are due to some unchangeable
> deficit in themselves, they lose hope and stop trying.
> The basic belief that leads to optimism, remember, is
> that setbacks or failures are due to circumstances that
> we can do something about to change them for the bet-
> ter.[7]

The "artful critique," as Goleman refers to it, is essential to building a forward-moving, successful business. That is the central value of the PPC approach (described in chapters 7 and 8). It is specific. It discusses what aspects of the idea or the job are good. It takes a look at the potential in the idea, the concept, or the new behavior, and only then deals with con-cerns. Yet it does so in a way that does not destroy the person or idea in the process, but instead provides a framework for building the idea or the concept. That's why the PPC technique is so valuable. No idea is perfect, but this tool gives leaders a method to provide a balanced approach to evaluation and creates an opening for a contributor to utilize her energy to overcome concerns about the idea and to develop it. The PPC technique gives the recipient valuable information about how to "do" the idea better; it does away with personal attacks.

HONOR THEM, REAP THE BENEFITS

Leader, it is absolutely imperative to honor the people who work for you. I assume you have hired the best people you can find, and unless they are volunteers, you are paying them. In return, your people are giving you days, weeks, months, and years of their lives to help you accomplish the goals, dreams, and objectives that you as a leader are creating.

Face it. You can't accomplish your goals without the people who work for you. The days of John Wayne cowboy-hero management are over. To succeed today you can't go it alone; you need the support of your entire team. Part of honoring the people who work for you is to be eager to listen to their ideas for improvement and to recognize and praise them for showing initiative in trying to solve company problems.

I believe most of us can relate to those times in our lives when we felt our creativity was valued. We recall fondly those periods when we tried new things in our organizations and were recognized for our efforts. Sure, we may have made mistakes, but even our errors helped us to be more effective and make some valuable contributions to the organization.

Creativity flourishes in an environment where praise is abundant. Leader, do you support your people with praise? Or do you destroy them with criticism? Your answer will go a long way toward determining whether your organization succeeds or fails.

Tootsie Rolls, Animal Crackers, and Other Odd Roads to Prosperity

———————

*In the managerial organization, the top people sit in judgment;
in the innovative organization it is their job to encourage ideas,
no matter how unripe or crude.*
PETER F. DRUCKER

About thirty years ago, the mayor of a suburb of Buffalo, New York, developed a vision for what his community could be like in the future. He wanted to capitalize on the close proximity of his city to the Buffalo area and to one of the seven wonders of the world, Niagara Falls. He researched his ideas thoroughly, examined the population base in the area, investigated the amount of tourist traffic, and concluded that the area could support a number of attractions.

Ideas in tow, he went to the city council and proposed several new ventures, including the construction of a wave pool, golf courses, a science center, and many other innovative plans for the community.

"No" came the overwhelming response of the city council. Among their comments:

* "It's too expensive."
* "We can't afford that now."
* "Our city is too small."
* "It will never work."
* "Your ideas are much too progressive for our community."

Years passed, and all of the things this mayor suggested

were adopted . . . in nearby communities. As a result of the common council's short-sightedness, millions of dollars of business and tax revenue went elsewhere.

Was the mayor a man ahead of his time? Probably. But leaders looking toward the future often have ideas that appear ahead of their time. In fact, a new idea by its very nature is ahead of its time. The main question is how to respond to those forward-looking ideas. While criticism may be the most common natural reaction, praise and recognition will accomplish a great deal more.

Just ask the communities which border a certain Buffalo suburb.

SUCKERS FOR PRAISE

Tom Peters and Robert Waterman, in their landmark book *In Search of Excellence*, drive this point home. They say that "all of us are self-centered suckers for a bit of praise and generally like to think of ourselves as winners. But the fact of the matter is that our talents are distributed normally. None of us is really as good as he or she would like to think, but rubbing our noses daily in that reality doesn't do us a bit of good"[1]

Peters and Waterman and George Leonard preach the same message when it comes to praise and recognition. In different ways, both tell managers to acknowledge the negative but accentuate the positive. Telling people what they're doing wrong while ignoring what they're doing right reduces their energy and eventually cuts into the company's profitability. When we talk about the importance of praise, we're really talking about finding ways to increase people's energy. This can't help but add to a firm's bottom line. Listen to Peters and Waterman once again:

> We all think we're tops. We're exuberantly, wildly irrational about ourselves. And that has sweeping implications for organizing, yet most organizations, we find, take a negative view of their people. They verbally berate participants for poor performance (most actually talk tougher than they act, but the tough talk nonetheless intimidates people). They call for risk taking but punish even tiny failures. They want an ovation but kill the

spirit of the champion. With their rationalist hats on they design systems that seem calculated to tear down their workers' self-image. They might not mean to be doing that, but they are. . . The lesson that the excellent companies have to teach is that there is no reason why we can't design systems that continually reinforce this notion. . . label a man a loser, and he'll start acting like one. . .

The systems in the excellent companies are not only designed to produce many winners, they are constructed to celebrate the winning once it occurs. Their systems make extraordinary use of non-monetary incentives. They are full of hoopla. . .

The old adage is, "nothing succeeds like success." It turns out to have a sound scientific basis. Researchers studying motivation found that the prime factor is simply the self-perception among motivated subjects that they are, in fact, doing well. Whether they are not, by any absolute standard, doesn't seem to matter much.[2]

Peters and Waterman admit that negative reinforcement—threats, punishment, etc.—produces results, but often in "strange, unpredictable and undesirable ways. . . It doesn't work very well, it usually results in frenetic, unguided activity." In fact, Peters and Waterman call it "usually a dumb tactic.[3]

Peters and Waterman ask readers to imagine they are being punished for failing to treat a customer well. The problem is that they still don't know what to do to receive approval; in fact, they might well respond by avoiding customers altogether, since they have "learned" that customers are associated with punishment. On the other hand, suppose someone in management tells them that a "mystery shopper" has complimented them on a job well done. How do you think they will respond? Probably by hurrying out to the floor to find more mystery shoppers to treat well. In this case, shoppers come to be associated with praise and recognition. The employee's self-esteem is built up and he senses that he is a winner.

The point is easily seen in such an imaginary scenario, isn't it? It looks so plain, so obvious. Yet how do most managers actually treat their workers? Peters and Waterman have a less than hopeful outlook:

> Our general observation is that most managers know very little about the value of positive reinforcement. Many either appear not to value it at all, or consider it beneath them, undignified, or not very macho. The evidence from the excellent companies strongly suggests that managers who feel this way are doing themselves a great disservice. The excellent companies seem not only to know the value of positive reinforcement, but how to manage it as well.[4]

The central question is this: How can a leader most effectively dispense praise and recognition? What are the best ways to accomplish this crucial function? Peters and Waterman offer six guidelines for effective use of praise and recognition.

1. *Make the praise specific.* Give as much content in your praise as possible.
2. *Make the praise immediate.* Thomas Watson, Sr., of IBM, is reported to have made a practice of writing out a check on the spot for notable achievements.
3. *The system of positive feedback in use should take account of achievability.* Small wins as well as major wins should be rewarded. Good news swapping is common in the excellent companies.
4. *A good portion of the positive feedback should come in the form of attention from top management.* This kind of reward may be intangible, but it may also be the most important form of recognition of all.
5. *Positive reinforcements should be unpredictable and intermittent.* Regular reinforcement loses impact because it comes to be expected.
6. *Recognitions should be smaller and more frequent rather than larger and more rare.* Big bonuses often discourage scores of workers who think they deserve them but can't get them; such big rewards frequently turn into political bomb shells.[5]

In general, leaders should simply remember to be generous with praise and stingy with criticism. It works!

A VERY "SOPHISTICATED" SYSTEM

Janet DiClaudio has served as Director of Medical Records at both Buffalo General Hospital in Buffalo, New York, and at Candler Hospital in Savannah, Georgia. While working at Buffalo General, Janet had trouble getting doctors to complete their medical records on time. Now, medical records are critically important. All medical procedures, however small, must be recorded. Medical records also determine how the hospital gets paid. Unfortunately, filling out medical records is not the most exciting thing in the world. It is not billable time, it is routine, detailed, and often very boring. Yet it must be done.

Janet solved her problem by developing a very "sophisticated system" to get doctors to complete their medical records on time. You might take special note of her solution just in case you need to motivate people to do some routine things they would rather not be doing.

Janet calls her system, "Tootsie Roll Pops." You know, the kind you buy in bags at the grocery store. Here's how it works.

Every time a doctor completes a medical record on time, she gets a Tootsie Roll Pop and her name goes into a drawing for a magnum of champagne. Now, some of these doctors can afford to *buy* a Tootsie Roll Pop factory and they have cases of the finest champagne back home in their wine cellars. Yet on the day of the first drawing for the magnum of champagne, there were twenty doctors in their scrubs and lab coats, Tootsie Roll Pops in their mouths, betting on who would win. And get this: Medical record productivity went from something like 42 percent completion to over 80 percent completion as a result of this campaign.

Several months after Janet left Buffalo and took a new position at Candler Hospital in Georgia, I asked how things were going for her. "Roger, the doctors are acting like children," she said, "so I've decided to treat them like children."

"Janet, what are you doing?" I asked.

"Well, we've gone through twenty pounds of animal crackers in the last two weeks," she replied.

"Janet! First it was Tootsie Roll Pops in Buffalo; now it's animal crackers in Savannah. What's going on?"

She explained that her new hospital had a backlog of about 300 medical records. To change that, she instituted a system which rewarded completed medical records from the backlog with a handful of animal crackers.

Two weeks and twenty pounds of animal crackers later, the hospital had only thirty-two medical records to complete, resulting in a collection of more than four and a half million dollars in attestation signatures (attestation signatures verify that the coding of the diagnosis and procedures in the medical record are correct. Then the bill can be processed.).

Not a bad investment, eh? Twenty pounds of animal crackers resulting in four and one half million dollars!

I call Janet the Queen of Employee Involvement; she constantly involves her staff in solving work related problems. When she eventually got doctors to complete their medical records on time, another problem emerged. The doctors weren't coming to the medical records office to sign them.

Janet gave that problem to her staff. In a Creative Problem Solving session she asked, "How might we get doctors to sign off on their completed medical records?" One idea her group conjured up was, "If the doctors aren't coming to medical records, let's take medical records to the doctors."

That idea at face value is a pretty far-fetched solution. Medical Records is an entire department of a hospital. You can't follow doctors around with an entire department. But Janet, as a leader, had established the environment in her organization in which people felt free to contribute their ideas. Although far-fetched, the idea was intriguing. The group tried Pluses, Potentials, and Concerns on the idea. In addition, they did a little research. It found that medical records was in one part of the hospital while a consistently high concentration of doctors was in another. Where were the doctors, do you suppose? In the doctors' lounge, of course.

So what was the answer? Move Medical Records to the doctors? Not quite. But why not put a desk from Medical Records in the hallway in front of the doctors' lounge, then staff it with a Medical Records staff person, two computers and a telephone?

These days, when the medical record is completed, it doesn't sit in the Medical Records offices, waiting for a doctor to come and sign it. Instead it is taken to the desk in the hallway in front of the doctors' lounge. Now when a doctor comes down the hall to the lounge for a cup of coffee or to a consult with a colleague, a Medical Records staff person recognizes the doctor, opens the appropriate record and asks the doctor if she could sign off on it. When she does, she gets a dinosaur graham cracker cookie.

Does the whole operation sound crazy to you? Think again!

All it cost to put the desk in the hallway was the expense of installing two phone jacks. But by moving a Medical Records outpost to a desk-in-the-hall-by-the-lounge, the hospital is regularly reducing its accounts receivable by about *three and one-half million dollars a month!*

One of the reasons Janet DiClaudio has been so successful in working with doctors is that she has an in-depth understanding of the working environment. She knows doctors aren't motivated by money or time. They usually have a good deal of money and very little time. The environmental factor that worked for her was recognition. Even doctors need recognition!

Recognizing people for a job well done doesn't have to be expensive. A dinner, a note, even Tootsie Roll Pops and animal crackers will work. And the payoff can be extraordinary.

RECOGNITION AND THE MOTIVATION TO EXCEL

Research on creative productivity has found that people are motivated by different things. It's a great mistake to think that money is the only motivator. In fact, a group I worked with in a public utility generated a list of fifty ways they would like to be recognized for their creative efforts. Four of those fifty items—less than 10 percent—had anything to do with money. Some of the creative rewards they craved included:

  ✳ Flexible schedule
  ✳ Time off
  ✳ Using the company president's office for a day
  ✳ A preferred parking place

✴ A ride in the company's hot air balloon
✴ Using a company car for a day

Some leaders have a hard time believing that money is not always the best motivator. They should pay close attention to the following story, related by Teresa Amabile of Harvard University, who conducted this research in collaboration with her colleagues at The Center for Creative Leadership:

> The chemist who had just arrived for his appointment looked no different from the others I'd been interviewing all day at this major R&D laboratory in a large chemical company. Over two dozen scientists had already answered my standard question: "Can you tell me about an example of high creativity from your work experience, as well as an example of low creativity?" The stories I'd been hearing were full of rich, intriguing detail. But I was completely unprepared for this man's startling remarks.
>
> "One thing I've done to stay creative is to cut my salary down, so management doesn't worry about what I'm doing every moment. Once a salary gets up there, management is forced to get involved in everything you do, because every moment of your time costs the company money. So I avoid this by turning down the raises. I'm here to have a good time. I have the joy of thinking... I love just thinking things over, just circling a problem. I am interested in things that don't work, and I even seek them out. When I see conceptual contradictions, I go get them. Just let me play. Give me a big enough playpen, and I'll go from there."
>
> Not surprisingly, I would later learn that this man's colleagues and supervisors considered him to be eccentric and difficult to manage. At the same time, though, they agreed that he consistently produced the laboratory's most creative work.
>
> Although of the 120 scientists my colleagues and I interviewed, he was the only one to say he refused salary increases, this man merely presents an extreme form of an attitude that we found quite prevalent among

the most creative participants: they are in it for the fun and the personal sense of satisfaction they get from meeting an intriguing challenge. If anything gets in the way of that fun and satisfaction–particularly constraints placed on them by their work environment–their level of creative productivity suffers.[6]

This account points out the type of motivation that spurs creative productivity. It isn't always money–in fact, most often it isn't. When a worker enjoys his or her work and is praised and recognized for noteworthy accomplishments, motivation skyrockets.

As a result of conducting hundreds of studies on adults and children, Amabile's research led to the "intrinsic motivation principle of creativity."[7] This principle states that people will be most creative when they feel motivated primarily by the interest, enjoyment, satisfaction, and challenge of the work itself and not by external pressures. In other words, people will be most creative when they are *intrinsically* motivated (motivated primarily by intrinsically interesting aspects of the work itself) and not *extrinsically* motivated (motivated primarily by goals outside of the work itself, such as supervisory restrictions, deadlines, or monetary rewards).

Intrinsic motivation is doing something because you love to do it. You would probably do this activity even if you weren't paid for it. Extrinsic motivation, on the other hand, is motivation for a reward outside of the task. Extrinsic motivation would include things like money, high grades in school, or a promotion.

Albert Einstein saw intrinsic motivation as conducive to creativity and outside pressure as detrimental to it. He said, "It's a very grave mistake to think that the enjoyment of seeing and searching can be prompted by means of coercion and a sense of duty."[8]

Arthur Schawlow, the Nobel Laureate in physics, said this about his own creativity and that of his colleagues: "The labor of love aspect is important. The successful scientists often are not the most talented, but the ones who are just impelled by curiosity."[9]

THE VALUE OF DIVERSITY

Adaptive and Innovative types of creativity are not the only differences to keep in mind when people work on problems. (See page 20.) Cultural diversity, diversity in expertise, and female and male viewpoints on situations are also important. As Dave Meier of the Center for Accelerated Learning emphasizes, capacity is diversity. Your organization will be able to deal with more and different kinds of challenges and opportunities, the more diverse it is.

The organizations we lead will be able to make dramatic, significant, and positive changes in the way we do business and create new products and services if we are able to utilize the strength of our diverse work force. Our culturally diverse work force is a powerful source of new and valuable information and can provide a strong base for more effective teams and participative organizational structures.

In the U.S., the work force today does not think, look, or act like the work force of the past. It does not hold the same values, pursue the same needs and desires, or have the same experiences of previous years. There are many more culturally diverse groups in the work force today as compared to the past when there were only a few visible ethnic groups. For example, half of the fifty-six million people who enter the labor force between 1990 and 2005 will be women. Because of changes in attitudes and values, there is a wider variety of lifestyles, motivations, and choices that were not apparent or even accepted in the past.

Leaders can view this diversity as a threat to control or as a wake-up call to creativity. For example, in a recent article in *Business Week*, "Diverse by Design," Alice Cuneo stated that "when you make a point of valuing other people's contributions, some good ideas for products make their way back to headquarters." She illustrated the marketing success that Levi Strauss had when it promoted diversity in its organization. Levi credits an Argentinean employee with thinking up its Dockers line of casual pants, now worth more than $1 billion a year.

Diversity can be viewed as an advantage if it is valued, nurtured, and well-managed. Of course, diversity is much more difficult to control, unless you have a process that harnesses diversity and channels it toward creating a result. One of the most powerful ways to nurture and value our diverse work force is to utilize a process like Creative Problem Solving to focus that diversity on solving problems and capitalizing on opportunities.

Leaders can help create these "labors of love" by liberal use of praise and recognition. Threats and appeals to duty and obligation are not nearly as effective in creating the results you want as are praise and recognition. I know that giving praise and recognition does not come naturally to many leaders. It may be that it's not an inherent part of your own nature. But if you want to succeed in the marketplace and keep ahead of your competitors, you'd better learn the value of praise, then practice it in your business. The bottom line is, it works.

That's the message that author George Leonard trumpets in his book *Mastery*. In speaking of the methods chosen by teachers and leaders to motivate those under them, he writes, "What doesn't work, despite a certain macho attitude to the contrary, is scorn, excoriation, humiliation—anything that destroys the student's confidence and self-esteem. Even the praise-stingy teacher must in some way show respect for the student in order to get long-term positive results. The best teacher generally strives to point out what the student is doing right at least as frequently as what she or he is doing wrong, which is just what UCLA coach John Wooden, perhaps the greatest basketball mentor of all time, managed to do all through his long, winning career. Wooden was observed to maintain approximately a fifty-fifty ratio between reinforcement and correction, with exceptional enthusiasm on both sides of the equation. . . "[10]

Of course, this principle doesn't apply only to the classroom and to the basketball court. It applies equally to the world of business. Tom Peters, whom Leonard calls "perhaps the nation's top management consultant," speaks of "an almost spooky similarity of language" among America's top company managers when it comes to praise and recognition. "To a man and woman," writes Leonard, "they stress the value of a positive attitude and the effectiveness of praise and other forms of positive feedback. 'The most successful managers,' Peters told me, 'are those who are unwilling to tolerate the negative stuff.'"[11]

PRAISE, PRAISE, AND MORE PRAISE

Janet DiClaudio has learned the value of praise and recognition so well that now she's writing articles on the topic. In an article titled "Praise, Praise and More Praise: Designing a Creative Environment in a Health Care Setting," Janet wrote:

> The employees in the department shuddered the first time I entered the room. What a welcome! My opening statement was "I am not here to do your jobs-I am here to get you what you need, so that you are able to do your jobs." It was obvious from my reception that I needed to communicate with them individually and in groups as soon as possible.[12]

During her first six weeks on the job, Janet conducted job clarification interviews with everyone in the department. Each interview took about an hour and had seven objectives. Those objectives were:

1. Identify each department member's job responsibilities
2. Identify likes and dislikes
3. Identify department members' skills and talents
4. Identify on-the-job problems
5. Request suggestions for improvement
6. Initiate a working relationship with each individual
7. Share my expectations with them

Janet designed questions for each department member to think about before coming in for an interview. The questions were printed in a questionnaire, on which Janet entered the interviewee's responses. Janet wanted to get an idea of each employee's job duties, those duties performed daily, weekly, biweekly, monthly, quarterly, and annually. Janet also wanted to know what all employees liked most and least about their jobs. She asked them to list any hindrances to performing their job as well as suggestions for solving each problem. Finally, she asked participants to list their hobbies and any additional questions, comments, or suggestions they might have.

After the interviews, the responses were tallied and summarized; results were submitted both to employees and the administration. Thirty-four problems were identified in the clerical section and another twenty-four in the transcription section. Very few problems overlapped. Responses were listed from the most to least frequent and then evaluated based on urgency. Problems ranged from the simple, such as distributing copies of the approved abbreviation list, to the complex, such as changing the social environment. The only unanimous request was to change the wallpaper (it was ugly, Janet admitted).

It became clear to Janet that communication was the key to success. Therefore she initiated monthly departmental business meetings and a monthly newsletter from her desk called *Off the Record.* "The newsletter was used to praise individual employees for their accomplishments, list important dates (e.g., weddings and meetings), and describe new or updated departmental systems," Janet wrote. "A copy was sent to the Community Relations Department, which then included appropriate material in the hospital-wide employee newsletter, *The Candlergram.*"[13]

In addition, department business meetings now include the introduction of new employees, important announcements, policy clarifications, and in-services on pertinent topics.

Of course, Janet did not always enjoy a perfect situation on the job. Eventually she had to institute some "creative progressive discipline" with a few employees. Yet the issues to be addressed in each disciplinary session were related in positive terms by the supervisor. For example, if an employee was absent frequently, the supervisor discussed attendance, not absenteeism. The employee might be told that although they were on the job 85 percent of the time, the goal was 95 percent of the time. In addition, "They are given an opportunity to make suggestions for improving their attendance record," Janet wrote. "Many people may be able to change the days of the week or the hours of the day on which they would be able to report to work. This is not possible in all cases, however. The employee and the supervisor may discover that the employee does not like his/her job and, if this is handled positively, he/she might transfer to a different position, even a different department, and do very well."[14]

Let's step back a moment and take a look at what Janet did in her role as a creative leader. First, she used her creativity skills and encouraged the development of creativity in her people. Instead of ignoring the department's problems, she created an environment in which people were unafraid to point out those problems. Second, she encouraged her employees to identify the problems that needed to be solved and to generate ideas to solve them. This gave them an application focus and thereby increased their commitment.

The result? Each problem was tracked by the person or persons who identified the problem and all fifty-eight problems were resolved within two years.

But that's not all. Two of the ideas chosen for implementation were contributed by the lowest paid individuals in the department, the filing clerks. One designed a new folder to house the department's permanent records, saving the hospital $80 per thousand, or a minimum of $2,400 per year. Another clerk saved the hospital a minimum of $600 in equipment (and an immeasurable amount of time) by suggesting a filing apron instead of shelf organizers for storing supplies and waste paper. The apron had two very large pockets (one for larger supplies and one for waste paper) and several smaller pockets for pens, pencils, scratch pads, and labels. It is made of soft polyester fabric and resembles a carpenter's apron. Janet, of course, loved the ideas. "If each of the employees in the department would save us $600" she wrote, "it would reduce our expenses by $26,000 per year!"[15]

THE POWER OF PRAISE

You simply can't go wrong by showering your employees and coworkers with praise. Of course, it must be genuine; who wants to receive an obviously bogus compliment?

But what power there is in generous, genuine praise! It has the muscle to give hope to the discouraged, energy to the feeble, and life to the dead. A letter that Ralph Waldo Emerson wrote to a young Wait Whitman encouraged the latter to finish and publish his now-famous book, *Leaves of Grass*. In part, that letter said, "I greet you at the beginning of a great career, which must yet have had a long foreground somewhere, for such a start. I rubbed my eyes a little to see if this sunbeam were no illusion: but the solid sense of the book is a sober certainty. It has the best merits, namely of fortifying and engaging." Emerson's public endorsement not only encouraged Whitman– "I was simmering, simmering," wrote Whitman, "Emerson brought me to a boil"–but helped the published book to sell out each printing.[16]

And beyond that, how much more effective is praise in helping your business to succeed than is crippling criticism!

ELEVEN

Make Mistakes – and Learn from Them

Living itself is a risky business.
If we spend half as much time learning how to take risks
as we spend avoiding them,
we wouldn't have so much to fear in life.
ANONYMOUS

Successful ideas often have this history;
They are advanced at least once unsuccessfully.
JOHN WILLIAMS

One of the IBM corporation's legends is built around an incident that occurred in its early years. It seems that a manager who worked for IBM's founder, Thomas Watson, Sr., lost ten million dollars for the company in a failed venture. The man thought that the only honorable thing to do was to commit organizational *hara-kiri*. He prepared his resignation and went in to see Mr. Watson.

The employee silently handed his resignation to Watson. Watson looked up, read the letter carefully, and promptly tore it to shreds. The astonished employee stared at Watson and asked, "I've just lost ten million dollars for this company—aren't you going to fire me?"

"Absolutely not!" Watson replied. "I've just spent ten million dollars on your education; you're much too valuable to this organization for me to let you go now."

TRIAL AND LEARN
Failure, mistake, fiasco, bomb, dud, flop, turkey, garbage, junk, reject, scrap, setback, breakdown, screw-up, blunder, blooper, foul-up, bungle, faux pas—these are just a few of the words that most of us use when things don't turn out the way we had planned or hoped or imagined. Look closely at those

words. They are all value judgments. They describe an outcome of an action in a decidely negative way.

Yet whenever you do anything, you create a result. A failure is simply a result that you hadn't anticipated. The expression "trial and error" focuses on unanticipated results that failed. But we rarely look at this unanticipated result in a positive way. We certainly don't describe it as a learning experience. If we look at failures as learning experiences, however, they can actually help us to become more successful. It is probably advisable to change the idea of "trial and error" into "trial and *learn.*"

Thomas Edison, it is said, experimented with about 6,000 ways to invent the lightbulb until he finally came up with the filament material that worked for him. Was each one of those initial combinations a failure? No, they just didn't produce the results Edison wanted.

LET YOUR EMPLOYEES DO THEIR JOBS BETTER
Some of you entrepreneurs and small business owners might find it difficult to stay out of your employees' way. After all, it is your business; you probably founded the company. But now the people who perform the jobs that make you successful know more about getting that job done than you do. So let them make it better!

During the time that Edison was trying to improve the electrical storage battery so he could store the electricity that powered his light bulbs, he had a conversation with one of his business investors. At this time in the project, Edison had tried about 50,000 things that didn't work. The investor gave this account of his conversation with Edison: "'Isn't it a shame that with the tremendous amount of work you have done, you haven't been able to get any results?' Mr. Edison turned on me like a flash, and with a smile retorted, 'Why, Man, I have got lots of results. I know several thousand things that won't work.'"

Edison was a master at using his mistakes as stepping stones to discovery. He lived out the maxim proclaimed by

Albert Szent-Gyorgyi: "Discovery consists of looking at the same thing as everyone else and thinking something different." There is much we could learn from him.

Never forget that mistakes can be stepping stones to success. So change your attitude about mistakes from trial and error, to trial and learn.

CHANGE YOUR ATTITUDE ABOUT FAILURE

All great leaders make mistakes. Creative geniuses make mistakes, too. They mess up, just like the rest of us. It was Joe Louis who said, "Everyone's got to figure to get beat sometime."

There is bad Beethoven. There are failed Picassos. There are incorrect theories by Albert Einstein. Duke Ellington would be the first to say that some riffs worked better than others. And, according to Joel Achenbach in a recent *Washington Post* article headlined, "When Genius Bombs," just because you are a great composer named Wagner doesn't mean that everything you do will be Wagnerian. Achenbach writes,

> Over time the master artist takes on the character of a super being, a cartoon genius. A piano is to Lizst as a hammer is to Thor, God of Thunder. We can imagine Beethoven composing by day and solving baffling murders by night. The problem with genius is that it doesn't give the great talents their due for working hard and plodding through difficult problems and taking chances and knowing which ideas to dump and which to deliver. Geniuses create the same way total ding-dongs create. Geniuses still have to put on their paint one stroke at a time.[1]

Achenbach continued, "Mistakes are integral to the process of creation. As the poet James Fenton said in a recent lecture at Oxford, the text of which was reprinted in the *New York Review of Books,* 'For a productive life, and a happy one, each failure must be felt and worked through. It must form part of the dynamic of your creativity.'"[2]

According to Dean Keith Simonton, a psychologist at the University of California at Davis and author of *Greatness: Who*

Makes History and Why, "Even outstanding people have phenomenal failures. That's why so many people don't achieve success, because the first time they fail they think they can't be successful. Creative geniuses stumble; they trip; they make horrible mistakes. Their highest and most acclaimed successes are constructed on the low rubble of humiliating failures."[3]

It is a fact that senior managers of innovative companies tend to view failure as the price of being innovative. They understand that their people will not stick out their necks for risky ventures if they know the ax will come crashing down on those same necks should they fail. Wise managers protect their creative workers from the fear of failure.

One company that has had a reputation for doing a good job of this is 3M. If a promising project fails for some reason, participants are not punished but are encouraged to try something else. They understand that if workers are threatened with dismissal after working on a failed project, they'll never try anything new again. At 3M, a worker involved in a failed project is given a new position–at the same level–somewhere else in the company. This has encouraged many employees to persevere despite setbacks–and has resulted in the creation of many new and successful products. Innovative companies, like 3M, reward their people for their efforts, not merely for results. Yet make no mistake–they get results! Sometimes this happens in the most amazing ways.

THEY ARE WATCHING YOUR FEET

If you want your people to be creative, then you have to be creative yourself. You have to let your people see you struggle with the tough issues and the crazy ideas and allow your employees to help you solve problems. You need to model the behavior you want to see in your employees. It doesn't matter what you think or intend or even say; what matters is how you behave. You may be saying one thing, but your people are watching your actions. You may be saying that you want some creative ideas, but whenever someone comes to you with a new idea you tell them all the things that are wrong with it. Don't expect any creative behavior from your people here, because your people are watching your feet. They will respond to what you do, your actions, not to what you say.

continued on page 169

continued from page 168
Unfortunately, in some organizations I have worked with, the leader doesn't understand that his actions are speaking so loudly that his employees can't hear a word he is saying.

THE STORY OF POST-IT NOTES

The Post-it note story is a classic in the creativity field. It centers around Arthur Frye, a chemical engineer at the 3M Corporation. Post-it notes began with a failure, a glue that didn't stick properly. This semi-sticky adhesive was originally developed by another 3M researcher, Spencer Silver. Now, at 3M, if a glue is a glue, it's supposed to stick like a glue, because quality is important. But what do you do with a semi-sticky adhesive that is only "temporarily permanent"? Enter Arthur Frye.

In addition to being a researcher at 3M, Frye sang in his church choir. He became frustrated with the small slips of paper he had to place in his hymnal to mark the page numbers of the songs during Sunday services. When he learned of Silver's semi-sticky adhesive, he asked him to apply some of it to a few slips of paper. Frye found the new invention worked marvelously well for holding his place in the hymnal. They stuck as long as he needed them to, but they would pull off without damaging the paper.

Frye believed he had a real product here, but he needed more than just the concept. So he approached the R & D department and Spencer Silver for a prototype.[4] With prototype in hand, Frye might have gone to the CEO or the Chairman, but he didn't. He thought that if he had the marketing department behind him, it might be easier to show the real authorities an opportunity they could not afford to pass up. Unfortunately, the marketing department was disinterested in his product. "What?" they asked. "A glue that doesn't stick all the time?"

But Frye remained undaunted. He decided to distribute sample Post-its to the people with the real power and opportunity to influence others: secretaries. Secretaries, he figured, could demonstrate the utility of the notes, and thus the need for the product. He began with the chairman's secretary. Soon other secretaries began calling her, asking about the handy little notes. Before long the requests became overwhelming. When the secretary called Frye for more, he directed her to the marketing depart-ment. Of course, it didn't take many requests from the chairman's secretary for marketing to catch on. They changed their minds and suddenly became interested–very interested. The rest, as they say, is history.

Marketing at 3M, by the way, took a lesson from Frye. When Post-its were finally introduced into the marketplace, the company began by sending samples to the CEOs' secretaries of all the Fortune 500 companies. The strategem worked.

This example shows how critical it is to understand how everyone in an organization might help in making a product successful. Frye was not only creative in his invention, but he continued to tap that creativity to get his idea accepted. He considered all the obvious people, but he held off for a more effective and creative solution. It paid off handsomely for him and the company.

One helpful way to think of failures is to consider them a good indication that the route we're on is probably not the most direct route to your goal. This is the real beauty of the Art Frye story. Not only did he take a glue that didn't stick properly–a failure in 3M's mind–but he also used his creativity to market the idea to people who weren't immediately receptive.

If you're leading on the creative edge, you need to be flexible in your approach to get an idea implemented and to get that idea out to the market. Coming up with ideas isn't enough. It's also important to be able to sort, refine, develop, and implement those ideas. And that's where Art Frye showed himself a real expert.

DON'T STOP CREATING

Whenever you do anything, you create a result. A failure is merely a result that you didn't anticipate. If we look at failures as learning experiences, they can actually help us to become more creative.

George Bernard Shaw believed in productivity. His

advice to everyone was to "just keep writing." The so-called creative geniuses of our time work hard. They're prodigious. It seems that they can't stop themselves from churning out work.

Thomas Edison couldn't stop inventing. Joyce Carol Oates couldn't stop writing. Shaw published fifty-five plays. Milton Avery created enough paintings to fill art galleries; when asked how he got inspiration, he said by going to the studio every day.

Leon Botstein, the composer, says you can't plan your breakthroughs; you just have to keep plugging away, and wait, and hope. "Breakthrough is not when you want it, it's not when you expect it," he said. "It's a function of the constant activity. It is only the constant activity that generates the breakthrough."[5]

It seems that when a creator creates most, the creator creates best.

As John Gardner in his book *On Leadership* emphasized, "The question is not 'Did you take a fall?' but 'Did you get up and continue?'"[6] Successful, creative people grow through criticism and failure. They know that the book of life has many chapters. As James Michener, the prolific, prize winning author once said, "I like challenge. I don't mind defeat. I don't gloat over victories. I want to stay in the ball game."[7] Dave Meier, Director of the Center for Accelerated Learning, sums up this philosophy when he says, "Anything worth doing is worth doing poorly at first."[8]

WATCH OUT!
The quality movement in this country has done remarkable things to strengthen the economic vitality of many companies. At the same time, it has begun to convince disgruntled Americans to buy American products again. One of the axioms of the quality movement is, "Do it right the first time, every time."

But watch out! That advice can bite your hand off if you run your business based totally on its guiding philosophy.

Don't get me wrong; doing things right is crucial. The problem comes when we use this quality principle *too early*. Let me explain. What tends to happen is that people try to "do it right the first time, every time" when they are generating ideas and attempting to solve problems. But that's the absolute worst time to "do it right." That is *the* time to make mistakes, and lots of them. Only by making many mistakes and learning from their unanticipated results will you be able to create the new products that can be done right the first time, every time.

Burt Rutan, the airplane designer who, along with his wife Jeana Yeager, built and flew the ultra light aircraft Voyager around the earth on one tank of gas, said this about failure: "I've got to develop nine prototypes that go nowhere to make one that goes into production for big money. Only the place that tolerates failure gives rise to the thinking that results in success."[9]

At least in the idea generation stage, mistakes are not to be avoided at all costs. It is those very mistakes that will enable you to succeed.

Creativity flourishes in an environment that says it's okay to make some mistakes, that it's okay to try some new things. Part of being creative is making mistakes.

THE MISTAKE QUOTIENT

One technique I use in my creativity seminars to help people feel comfortable and allow themselves to experiment with new ways for solving tough problems is to give each one of them a "mistake quotient." I assure them that they have at least thirty mistakes to make . . . and if they make thirty mistakes, I'll give them thirty more. It is amazing how participation increases when people realize they won't be ridiculed if their idea flops or their performance comes out less than perfect.

So don't be so hard on yourself. Many of the most creative and effective people of our time have made some major blunders. Give yourself permission to make a few mistakes. Remember, if you're not making *some* mistakes, you're not making *any* discoveries.

Take a cue from the world of children's stories. Try looking at a mistake as if it were the frog that turned into a handsome prince. Sure, it's not what you expected. It won't win any beauty pageants. Its eyes bulge out, its skin is rough and green, it eats flies and its croaking can keep you awake at night. But if you embrace that ugly frog—and even kiss it!— you'll suddenly see the little creature transformed into your personal ticket to the Magic Kingdom . . . and you'll live happily ever after.

Okay, so maybe not "ever after." But I guarantee you'll be a lot happier than the guy who lies awake all night, worrying about a back yard full of frogs croaking their little lungs out.

TWELVE
Trial and Error,
or Trial and Learn?

The way to succeed is to double your failure rate.
THOMAS WATSON, JR., FORMER PRESIDENT OF IBM

One of my favorite video offerings is a series called "The Search for Solutions." This unique series profiles not only some of the most important inventions in history, but also describes the hard work, determination, and willingness to make mistakes that characterize most crucial innovations. In the video *Trial and Error,* the announcer intones in a deep, sonorous voice:

> You try something new. So, it doesn't work. At least you know what not to do. Some call it "trial and error." But it's more like "trial and learn." If it's never been done before, how else can you figure it out? So you keep plugging. Who knows? Maybe you'll get something that flies.[1]

It's precisely that willingness to keep plugging even in the face of failure that leads to great discoveries. Often it is the mistakes themselves that open the door to wonderful and helpful innovations. That was certainly true about Wilhelm Konrad Roentgen, the discoverer of the X-ray. Another video in "The Search for Solutions" series profiles Roentgen and his extraordinary discovery—and asks some intriguing questions about failure and success.

If you suddenly found that you could see through a solid wall, would you believe your eyes? Friday night, November 8, 1895, German physicist Wilhelm Roentgen goes to his laboratory. He needs a darkened room for some experiments using a cathode ray tube, a device whose electrical properties have puzzled physicists for more than 30 years. As he turns on the tube, a piece of fluorescent paper nearby begins to glow. Some sort of radiation seems to be coming from the tube. But the tube is completely shielded in black cardboard; no light can leak out. What Roentgen saw was impossible, according to the physics of his day. Other scientists who worked with cathode ray tubes noticed that photographic plates in nearby cabinets became fogged, but instead of wondering why, they complained to the plate manufacturers.

A fact, out of context, is a nuisance to most people. Rather than find a home for it, they turn away. But not Roentgen. Asked later what he thought about on that momentous night, Roentgen gave a classic reply: "I didn't think. I investigated."

He takes pictures of his own hand. He sees what no one has ever seen before: Bones, inside living flesh. The discovery is given a name: X-rays. "X" for "unknown:"

To most people, a fact out of context is a nuisance. It's oftentimes treated as a failure. Yet what failures do is give us new information. It's critically important to look closely at those failures, because it is such "failures" that often lead to new insights and powerful new directions.

WHEN YOU'RE THREATENED

Realize that, as a leader, you might be threatened by innovative or radical ideas. Those ideas probably don't fit your current view of the world. Give these ideas your attention. They might be the ideas that will create the new products or services that will insure the future of your organization.

BUT I'M TOO OLD!
When you see the phrase, Creative Problem Solving, what images come to mind? What words occur to you? When I ask that question in my seminars, I hear all sorts of things. "Something that someone decided was unsolvable before." "Brainstorming." "I can't do it." Many times people see the phrase like this: Creative PROBLEM Solving.

Frankly, I struggle with the label Creative Problem Solving, because if you look at the word "problem" in the dictionary, you find this definition: "An obstacle encountered; uncertainty; perplexity." In other words, something that you don't want to have. And if somebody else has a problem, you usually don't want to get any of it on you.

Most of us look at problems as if they were to be avoided at all costs. But I'd like you to look at Creative Problem Solving with a fresh pair of eyes. Try thinking of Creative Problem Solving as Creative *Opportunity Finding.*

I do a lot of seminars and workshops for people in many organizations, and I get incredible excuses why people can't be creative. "I'm too old to be creative." "My job doesn't allow me to be creative." "If I ever had a creative idea, my brain would get a cramp." I always challenge those assumptions and arguments about why people can't be creative. Often I begin my challenge by reading the biography of someone I call a Creative Opportunity Finder. A piece of it goes something like this:

> I attended high school for a time, but I dropped out to become a jazz pianist. I did some radio work for a while, sold some real estate in Florida, but the bottom fell out. In the winter of 1926, I was stone broke. I didn't have an overcoat, a topcoat, or a pair of gloves. I drove into Chicago on icy streets. When I got home, I was frozen stiff, disillusioned, and broke. So I went back to being a salesman for the Lily Tulip paper cup company, worked real hard, and I became its midwestern sales manager. And in 1937, I came upon this new invention, this little machine that could mix five milkshakes at once. So I started a company to sell these multi-mixers, and in 1954 I

discovered that there was a small restaurant in San Bernardino, California, that had eight of my multi-mixers. And when I visited the place, I found that they were doing a tremendous business selling hamburgers, french fries, and milkshakes.

Of course, you know how this story ends. The gentleman's name was Ray Kroc; he founded the MacDonald's restaurant chain. The interesting thing about Ray Kroc is that he was fifty-two years old when he came across Dick and Mac MacDonald in San Bernardino, California, selling hamburgers, french fries, and milkshakes. So if a fifty-two-year-old paper cup salesman from Chicago can found the world's largest fast-food chain, those arguments of "I'm too old to be creative," and "my job doesn't allow me to be creative" just have to be thrown out the window.

The idea that creative people live with such intensity that they burn out and die young is actually a myth. The reality is that our creative lives often *prevent* us from dying young. Melanie Brown in her book *Attaining Personal Greatness* reported:

> The always productive Picasso died at ninety one. . . Michelangelo designed St. Peter's Church when he was almost ninety; Matisse's famous paper cutouts were a new art form he developed at age eighty-one; Henri Rousseau painted his most famous jungle pictures at sixty five. . . Goethe wrote *Faust*, Sophocles wrote *Oedipus*, and Verdi composed *Otello* and *Falstaff*, all when they were eighty or older. . . Longitudinal studies—those that follow the same people over a long period of time—clearly show that intellectual abilities of healthy people grow greater through the years rather than less.[3]

The lesson, the more we use the brain, the more it grows and keeps us growing—so keep creating!

BUT I'M AFRAID OF MAKING MISTAKES!

Often it's not age that stops people from tackling some

problem, but the frightening idea that they might fail. But what is failure? Failure is merely an indicator that you are moving to a new level. It's more like a "Yield" sign than a "Stop" sign. It's an invitation to move ahead, but with caution and with your eyes wide open.

Think of it like this. Whenever you learn a new skill, you are not going to be perfect at it at first. Otherwise, how would it be a learning experience? Remember when you started to ride a bicycle? You didn't succeed immediately, did you? Of course not. You fell down. But was it a failure? Did you stop trying to ride that bike? Of course you didn't. You got up, dusted yourself off, and hopped back on. Why? Because you wanted to ride that bike. You saw your end goal, that compelling image of you sailing down the hill in your neighborhood.

Failure gives you valuable information that you didn't have before you made that attempt. It's the same way in business as it is in other areas of life. Research has found that before entrepreneurs succeed at some venture, they fail on average *at least* three times in other ventures. Even though those failures could be incredibly painful, those who persisted learned valuable lessons about what to do and what not to do.

Quick rewards in business are the exception, not the rule. For most of us, the road ahead will seem endless and will feature plenty of set-backs along the way. It takes long hours of diligent work, readjustment, and setbacks to be successful. Yet those who persevere eventually succeed.

CREATE OPPORTUNITIES TO ALLOW YOUR EMPLOYEES TO CREATE

Think about what normally happens when you hire new employees or recruit new volunteers. Their first question tends to be, "What would you like me to do?" We then set out very carefully to tell them exactly what they should do. Closely following that first question is likely, "How do I do what I am supposed to do?" So once again we very quickly tell them exactly how to do their job. Their next question might be, "What are my tools and systems?" or

continued on page 180

continued from page 179
"What is going to help me do my work?" Again we give them the "correct" answers.

According to my colleague and friend, Ken Kumiega, international management consultant and President of World Class Business, what we have now created is a static system in which the employee does only what she has been told. As a result, she keeps repeating the process without change or growth. This continues until someone comes along and changes the procedure. Rarely does anyone appear asking for ideas for change or improvement—unless, of course, something goes wrong. The improvement necessary to make the job more effective is seen as someone else's responsibility, not the person doing the job. As a result, the employee eventually shuts off her thinking and checks her brain at the door as she checks in to work.

What is usually not done with new employees is to explain to them that this is just the initial way to do the job; their insight for making the job more effective is welcomed and expected. As part of their job, they will be taught creative problem solving skills they can use to change, advance, or create a completely different way to do their work.

A recent edition of *Success* magazine profiled five business people who overcame devastating setbacks to once again become leaders in their respective fields. The article led off with the story of Karl Eller, whom the magazine described as "one of the most powerful businessmen in the country, revered and feared throughout the West."[4] Yet it hasn't always been that way. Eller's tale, like those of the other four entrepreneurs profiled along with him, "is a tale of sensational success, ignominious defeat, and brilliant recovery. Each of our entrepreneurs was, at some point, utterly crushed. In the end, every one of them triumphed through self-confidence, force of will, unrelenting optimism, and unbelievable persistence. One of the lessons their lives teach: For an entrepreneur, strong ideas and inner strength are more important than possessing millions of dollars. . . Hardship teaches entrepreneurs that they themselves are the critical resource. Their contacts, skills, and above all, *attitudes* can overcome the most devastating defeats—and result in glorious victory.[5]

SIX GUIDELINES FOR UNLEASHING ENERGY

Deanna Berg, in her article: "Unleashing energy and enthusiasm: Learn from the masters of motivation," stated that creative leaders, especially those leaders who empower others, follow these six guidelines.[10]

Clarity: It is easier for people to feel empowered [and to express their creativity] when leaders are clear about what is expected, as well as how these outcomes relate to overall departmental or organizational performance.

Commonality: Leaders who empower others view their followers as partners, not subordinates. Develop shared visions of the desired future of your organization. These visions should also be compatible with personal visions and goals.

Communication: Create a structure for ongoing communication. Listening respectfully to diverse opinions is one of the most empowering things a leader can do.

Continuous learning: Give people all the information they need to make informed decisions. This might include financial reports, strategic plans, market analyses, and any skills or knowledge that would improve their ability to do their jobs.

Caring: People feel energized and enthused when they feel important and valued and when they believe they are making meaningful contributions. Caring is communicated when people are provided with resources, appreciation, and recognition.

Creativity: Rules need to be changed quickly in the rapidly changing business environment. Encourage people to challenge the status quo and give up the desire to be seen as "in charge." Question the value of all rules and restrictions that may demonstrate mistrust, waste time, and unnecessarily decrease people's freedom, spontaneity and responsibility.

Briefly consider Eller's personal history. He built the Circle K convenience store chain into a $3.5 billion enterprise, then lost it all. By the time Circle K filed for Chapter 11 bankruptcy protection in May 1990, Eller had lost millions. At age sixty-two he was flat broke and was even unable to collect severance pay.

Yet two years later, "he engineered a brilliant, no-money-down deal" in which (with the backing of a Canadian bank) he bought a Phoenix bill-board company for $20 million, "then spun the deal on a dime, selling off half to another buyer. He never had to put up a single dollar."[6] In early 1996, he bought a Chicago outdoor advertising company valued at $500 million. Eller's new corporation, Eller Media Co., owns 43,000 billboards across the country and expects revenues of $250 million this year. Eller now runs the biggest outdoor advertising company in the nation-at sixty-seven years of age.

"Failure's good for you," Eller says. "It teaches you lessons. I guess the reason I didn't fold up my tent is because a guy like me goes through life, takes a lot of chances, and has failures. I didn't want to go down in the history books as a failure."[7]

Eller points out a crucial key: failure is good for you, but you don't want to live there. Don't be afraid of failure, but don't marry it, either. Both extremes will lead to disaster.

THE FAILURE HALL OF FAME
Some of the most famous, most revered names in history have also carried a long list of failures in their personal biographies. In fact, one of our most celebrated heroes also endured some of the most hardship. Perhaps you recognize his vita, which is often used to illustrate this point:[8]

When he was seven years old, his family was forced out of its home on a legal technicality, and he had to work to help support family members. At the age of nine, his mother died.

At twenty-two, he lost his job as a store clerk. He wanted to go to law school, but his education wasn't good enough.

At twenty-three, he went into debt to become the owner of a small store.

At twenty-six, his business partner died, leaving him a huge debt that took years to repay.

At twenty-eight, after courting a girl for four years, he asked her to marry him. She said no.

At thirty-seven, on his third try, he was elected to Congress, but two years later, he was turned out of office.

At forty-one, his four-year-old son died, and it broke his heart.

At forty-seven, he failed again, this time as the U.S. vice-presidential candidate.

At forty-nine, once more he ran for the Senate, and lost.

At fifty-one, he was elected president of the United States. His name? Abraham Lincoln, a man many consider the greatest leader this country has ever had.

LEARN FROM FAILURE
If only we would learn the difference between "trial and error" and "trial and learn"! Consider the invention of chemotherapy:

> Sometimes, pioneers set out with nothing but a hunch. Back in 1901, an immunologist named Paul Ehrlich had the idea that man-made chemicals might search out specific germs in the body and kill them. A "magic bullet," he called it. Doctors called him crazy. In his laboratory, professor Ehrlich tried chemical compounds, one by one on diseased animals—a laborious process. He tried 10; he tried 50; 100; 300. Finally, years later, number 418 gave him his first positive answer. It killed the infection. It also killed the mouse. But now, Ehrlich could narrow his search. He started trying all the chemical variations related to Compound 418. Then, at try 606 [he came across] a compound he called "Salvarsan." It killed the infection and spared the mouse. Salvarsan became the first real cure for syphylis. Other man-made chemicals would be identified as disease fight-

ers. Medicine had a new arsenal. Chemotherapy was born.[9]

Once again, this example illustrates that there is a very big difference between trying and failing. The key is to keep on trying, even as you look carefully at the failures. It's those "failures" that give us valuable information.

LOOKING GOOD, BUT DOING POORLY
Probably one of the biggest obstacles to leaders risking failure is the desire to "look good." We all have a tendency to try to keep up appearances even if it means denying the truth or sacrificing future opportunities. Yet this is so counterproductive.

Think of a Most Valuable Player candidate in the major leagues. No matter how good he might be, the time inevitably comes when he misjudges a fly ball and crashes to the turf—in front of millions of fans. Now, if he's willing to do that, shouldn't we be willing to take a few pratfalls of our own? If we are always worrying about how we're going to appear to onlookers, we'll never reach the levels of concentration that are essential if we are to learn and achieve noteworthy performances.

How can you move toward mastery in leading on the creative edge? One big key is to value mistakes. Don't be afraid of them. If you aren't making mistakes, you aren't trying anything new—which means you're stagnated. And that's never a good thing in the highly competitive business world of today.

So keep trying. Encourage your employees and coworkers to keep at it. Create an environment that encourages the taking of risks. Reward people for their efforts; don't punish them for their failures. That's when breakthroughs take place. That is why it is so important to encourage the small ideas that create incremental improvement in the organization. By valuing and implementing those small, incremental changes—many of which come through mistakes and failures—you set the stage for new breakthroughs to occur.

It is highly unlikely and almost absurd to think that

a new breakthrough will occur in an organization that doesn't make room for failure. I have often worked with organizations that want the big breakthrough with the potential to turn the company around. Let me revise that: Most of them don't want the "big" breakthrough, they want the "fairy-tale" breakthrough. They want what they're unable to achieve.

The truth is, if the big breakthrough ever occurred in such a company, its leaders probably wouldn't recognize it. By fearing and avoiding mistakes and failures, they have for all practical purposes ruled out the kind of new, thinking and innovation that alone give birth to breakthroughs.

Do you want your company to succeed? To achieve a distinct advantage in the marketplace? Then heed the advice of Elbert Hubbard, who maintained, "The greatest mistake a man can make is to be afraid of making one." You can make a lot of mistakes, but don't make that one. It's the one mistake that's a killer.

THIRTEEN

You Set the Environment

———⊐+◈+⊏———

Innovative organizations provide freedom to act,
which (in turn) arouses the desire to act.
ROSABETH MOSS KANTER,
AUTHOR OF *THE CHANGE MASTERS*

The hospital had scheduled a day-long training program in Creative Problem Solving for managers and supervisors. It paid my fee, my airfare, and my hotel accommodations. It also paid the salaries of all 100 people who were in the seminar. This was an expensive day! The director of training and organizational development introduced me to the chief administrator of the hospital, who in turn introduced me to the staff.

"Ladies and gentlemen, Dr. Firestien is here today to help us become more creative and to give us some important tools to help us solve our problems in new and innovative ways. Today is important. These methods are designed to jump start our total quality program. Dr. Firestien tells me this is going to be a very interactive program. So please get involved; and please use these methods beyond today as you return to your work tomorrow. And now without further ado. . ."

I walked up to the front of the room, thanked the chief administrator for his kind introduction, and showed the first slide.

Five minutes later the CEO left the room and was not seen for the rest of the day.

The seminar went well. People learned creativity skills they could use at the hospital and in their personal lives. I closed the session and asked participants to fill out the evaluation forms. After everyone left the room, the director of training and I discussed the day and reviewed the feedback. One theme kept coming up again and again:

"Good session. My boss should have been here."

"Why didn't the CEO stay?"

"The board of directors needs to be trained in this. Why didn't they attend the seminar?"

"I really want to use this stuff, but I don't know if my boss would understand."

"Where were all the senior managers?"

Hospitals aren't the only corporations that suffer from such short-sightedness. I have seen the same situation replay itself endlessly with schools, banks, and manufacturing firms.

Consider what happened at the hospital. The leader sent several important messages:

1. He is much too busy to spend any time in training or in improving his skills.
2. He knows all this stuff already; besides, it is his people who need to get fixed.
3. He doesn't need to be creative, but his people do.
4. While this training is simply not worth his valuable time, his employees need to sit through every bit of it.

The result? Chances are nil that his people will apply and use these methods for more than a few weeks after the program ends. The leader's absence clearly shows how little upper management values this type of training. He doesn't realize it, but he is effectively sabotaging any chance of getting these methods implemented in the workplace. Why? Because the leader is now "process illiterate." His people know more about the creative process than he does, so when they come to him with improvement ideas, he won't know how to deal with them. Worse yet, he will deal with these ideas the way he has always dealt with them: He will tell his employees all the reasons why their new ideas won't work. Very quickly his people will understand that he is not at all interested in doing things differently or solving problems in new ways.

The leader's behavior in essence trains his employees not to participate, not to apply anything they learned in the seminar. While the words may never come out of his mouth, nevertheless he shouts to his employees, "Just do your work the way it has always been done-oh yes, and give me a creative idea when I need it."

Yet another expensive day spent in training with little or no return.

THE LEADER'S INFLUENCE

Unsurprisingly, it is the leader who has the single most important influence on an organization's environment for creativity. The leader's behavior is the major influence in determining whether an organization will grow to be successful, creative, cutting edge, innovative ... or stagnate and die.

THE MYTH OF THE LONE INVENTOR

One myth that blocks our creativity is that of the lone inventor toiling away in his attic or garage. It is easy to name who invented the airplane or the light bulb or the telephone.

But who invented the jumbo jet, or the silicon chip, or the 800 inward WATS number or the fax machine, or the video cassette recorder, or the laptop computer? One of the reasons why most of us can't name these inventors is that they weren't just one person. They were teams of people in organizations. For our organizations to become more creative, it is crucial that we work together as teams to effectively generate and evaluate ideas.

In a study conducted by Goran Ekvall at public dental services in Stockholm, Sweden, the effects of leadership styles on the climate for creativity were examined.[1] In this study, eighty-five clinics participated. Each clinic had from ten to forty employees and was managed by a dentist. The three leadership styles examined were:

1. An orientation to change and development
2. An employee relations orientation
3. A task and organizational structure orientation.

Ekvall found a strong relationship between leadership style and climate. The change and development-oriented leadership style encouraged the support of new ideas, dynamism and liveliness, debates and risk taking. The employee relations style fostered trust and openness and minimized conflicts. On the other hand, a task/structure leadership orientation did none of these things. Key lesson: *the leadership behaviors in bureaucratic, highly structured, and controlling organizations do not foster an environment that nurtures creativity.*

Once again, Ekvall's study makes it clear that the leader is the single most important factor in creating an organizational environment that nurtures creativity or destroys it. Leader, it is in your power to create an environment that encourages employees to take risks, to try new approaches, to make your company successful. Conversely, your attitudes and actions can stifle and even eradicate these elements from your business, thus gravely injuring your opportunities for success in the marketplace.

This naturally brings up the question, what is an organizational environment for creativity? Does it honestly make a difference in creative productivity? And if it does make a difference, what can you do about it?

AN ENVIRONMENT FOR CREATIVITY

Most people I talk to have a pretty good idea of those times in their organizational life when they were involved, excited, motivated, and creative. They also have a pretty good idea when they were demoralized, demotivated, bored, and stressed-out.

When I ask students in my university classes to describe a particularly creative time in their organizational life, they often describe either a great class they had in college in which the teacher provoked their thinking and got them excited and involved in the subject, or a great job in which they felt they really contributed to the work. They describe these situations with phrases like the following:

∗ "I was allowed a lot of freedom."
∗ "I was allowed to be flexible in doing things."

★ "I participated in forming the goals I was to meet."
★ "The group I worked with supported my ideas."
★ "I felt free to try new things."
★ "I felt valued by my peers and supervisors."
★ "I felt relaxed and at ease."
★ "We had fun."

When I ask these students to describe a work or educational situation in which they were very uncreative or learned very little and were barely involved, they used these phrases:

★ "There was no trust."
★ "I felt confined."
★ "There was a lot of conflict."
★ "My boss was not open minded."
★ "There was no order or organization."
★ "I had no support from my coworkers."
★ "It was a stressful place that was out of control."
★ "There were lots of rumors and gossip."
★ "I was not allowed to voice my opinions."
★ "I felt my ideas were not valued."
★ "There was a lot of ridicule."
★ "I was bored."

Every one of my students agreed that organizational environments which valued them, allowed them freedom to try new things, and encouraged them to contribute their ideas, improved their performance.

EKVALL'S CLIMATE FOR CREATIVITY QUESTIONNAIRE
Is it possible to measure an environment that nurtures creativity? You bet. That's just what Dr. Goran Ekvall has done in developing the Climate for Creativity Questionnaire (CCQ).[2] We'll investigate this valuable questionnaire more thoroughly in the next chapter, but for now let's at least get some picture of what it does.
    The CCQ consists of fifty items and is designed for use by a department, a division, or an entire company to

provide a profile of the organization over ten dimensions. The instrument is designed to do a number of things—such as, getting information from organizational members on how open they believe the organization is to creativity, working together as teams, freedom to try new ideas, and dealing effectively with conflict.

I've seen the CCQ used in a couple of ways. Sometimes it's used at the beginning of an intervention to "trouble shoot" the organization's environment. As a result, we've been able to structure programs designed to increase or enhance aspects of the organization that the CCQ demonstrated were weak. For example, we've been able to design programs to help increase trust in various divisions, to help provide methods and techniques for people to develop ideas more effectively, and to provide advice on how to get more time to develop those ideas.

The CCQ also compares the organization with other organizations that have been rated as innovative (as determined by patents and productivity) or stagnated (regarding their inability to create new products and get those products to the marketplace). We'll look more closely at the difference between innovative and stagnated organizations in the next chapter.

We've also used the CCQ to assess how well a creativity program has done in the organization. We've used the questionnaire before delivering training and suggesting some changes in the organizational structure, as well as using the CCQ after an intervention to address the weak areas pointed out by the CCQ.

Essentially, the CCQ takes the "temperature" of an organization regarding its willingness to accept new ideas, to allow people to work on those ideas, and then to put those ideas into action in the marketplace. It provides the leader with a profile of her organization, suggesting areas that could use some enhancement or that could benefit by removing some blocks, or how to better structure the organization for innovation.

OTHER IMPORTANT VARIABLES

A host of organizational variables influence the environment for creativity in organizations. According to Ekvall, one of those variables is organizational structure. Studies on organizational structure and their relationship to the climate for creativity have included the following four types of structures:[3]

  1. *Centralization:* Such an organization is highly controlled by top management. It is characterized by one-way communication and narrow, specific delegation.

  2. *Formalization:* Such an organization has a strict and comprehensive system of written rules, intricate decision procedures and communication lines determined by the channels on the organizational chart. It is a typically constraining bureaucracy.

  3. *Order and plainness:* Such an organization is typified by unambiguous organizational roles, requirements, instructions, responsibilities, schedules, and plans. It is, however, a supportive bureaucracy.

  4. *Goal clarity:* Such an organization clearly communicates the vision, goals and strategies of the organization as a whole, all through its various departments and divisions.

  Various studies have found that centralization brings conflicts. It is no surprise, then, that highly centralized decision systems are associated with climates that restrict creativity and innovation.

  Formalization has a similar effect on the creative climate. No surprise again. The objective of a bureaucratic organization is to achieve stability and standardization and avoid flexibility and change; therefore, creativity suffers.

  Order and plainness is a bit more supportive and less constraining than the previous systems, yet it's more complicated to analyze. It provides challenge, support for new ideas and an environment of trust and openness and little conflict. Yet there doesn't seem to be a great deal of individual freedom in this system, even though some studies suggest it can foster risk-taking.

  Ekvall and his colleagues put forth a possible hypothesis for these apparently contradictory findings. It might be that order and plainness in an organization create an environment favorable to incremental innovation or improvement of existing products and processes, but when it comes to radical innovation—even in a climate with many favorable aspects—the organizational structure might still be too confining.

In most of Ekvall's studies, goal clarity generally improves an organization's creative climate. Yet other studies cast doubt on that conclusion. Ekvall found some very innovatively productive organizations with high creative climate scores which yet rated low on goal clarity. One might infer that these organizations might be even more creative if they had clearer goals; but it might equally be inferred that the unclear goals actually contributed to the climate that made radical innovation possible. Perhaps those unclear goals allowed employees the freedom to experiment and helped to create discussions about goals and strategies.

ENVIRONMENTAL STIMULANTS AND OBSTACLES TO INNOVATION

Teresa Amabile of Harvard University has identified nine factors that are environmental stimulants to creativity and innovation.[5] The numbers in parenthesis indicate the percentage of interviewees (research and development scientists) mentioning the factor. (See page 201)

EFFECTIVE ORGANIZATIONAL STRUCTURES

Part of creating an environment for creativity is the way an organization is designed. If we want to create organizations that foster our thinking and nurture our souls, then we need to look at how we design them.

So what kind of organizational structure supports creativity and learning? Dave Meier uses the diagrams on page 195 to chart the evolution of organizations from the pre-industrial through the industrial to the post-industrial.[4] It is in the post-industrial design, according to Meier, that the most learning (and hence the most creativity) is likely to occur.

Pre-Industrial

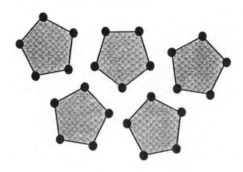

Industrial

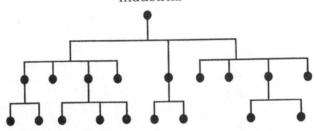

Post-Industrial

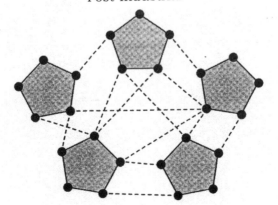

In the pre-industrial era the family business was the established form of organizational design. For example, thatchers in England made thatched roofs. There were cobblers, butchers, and farmers–all family businesses. No training department existed to manage training, nor were there seminars to attend or workshops in which to participate. If you wanted to learn a trade, you needed to "hang out" with someone who knew that trade.

Guild halls were ideal for this. You could literally hang around with people in the guild hall as they worked at their trade. You might apprentice to a "master" tradesman and increase your skills by helping him. People willingly helped each other in the guild halls. Competition hardly existed and as a result mentoring and cross-fertilization of ideas abounded.

The dawning of the industrial age hailed the beginning of the bureaucratic organization. As a result, organizations became compartmentalized and specialized. The Industrial Age did produce a great deal of wealth, but in the name of short-term profit it also initiated the extreme exploitation of the earth and of human beings. In this mechanized life, everything is compartmentalized and the worker is basically muscle, not mind. The mind resides upstairs, in management. Management tells workers what to do and what to think. Management has the vision, not you. All you have to do is buy into the vision as it is stated on the poster tacked on the wall.

Unfortunately, the bureaucratic organization also spawned individual competition to rise up the organizational ladder. To rise in the hierarchy, a man had to beat out those to his left and right; only the strong survived. As a result, organizational politics drained a great deal of creative energy from everyone.

In compartmentalized organizations, training or learning becomes a staff function that in many cases fails to penetrate or positively influence the whole organization. Teams usually don't work in an organization like this because individual competition is the only way to be rewarded.

According to Meier, in the post-industrial era most

jobs require mind and spirit (rather than muscle) in order to function. The reptilian-brained employee (discussed in chapter 9) is becoming a thing of the past. In this era, we can't treat people as though they have no feelings or ideas. Organizations today need employees' minds, their creativity, and their loyalty—in other words, their whole selves.

My own experience teaches me that people are ready for this change. They are ready for self-managed teams. They are ready to take responsibility for creating, not just doing what someone else says they should do, but adding their unique value to an organization. According to Meier, learning is the creation of value, and organizations that really learn are organizations where everyone has a chance to create value. The post-industrial design features teams of people working together in a collaborative way, building on their unique expertise to create value.

ENVIRONMENTAL OBSTACLES TO CREATIVITY AND INNOVATION

In addition to environmental stimulants to innovation, Teresa Amabile of Harvard University also found a number of environmental obstacles to creativity and innovation. In general, those obstacles include: Inappropriate reward systems in the organization, excessive red tape, a corporate climate marked by lack of cooperation across divisions and levels, and little regard for innovation in general. A listing of those organizational constraints is on page 202. Once again, the numbers in parentheses indicate the percentage of interviewees mentioning that factor.

Interconnected teams are designed around how work is actually done. Rarely does work occur in a linear format; normally it goes back and forth. Work occurs in a linear format only in an assembly-line type of organization. In today's information-driven companies, however, work seldom (if ever) occurs in a linear format. Instead, it occurs in an integrative and interactive environment. People *have* to talk to each other.

For example, I know of one organization that has

designed its work environment with this principle in mind. A large conference table is surrounded by cubicles. Whenever workers need to meet, they meet at the conference table in the center. If someone in a cubicle overhears a comment at the table about a project, he is free to interrupt, to get involved, and to add his input to the loop.

Organizations that have successfully used interconnected teams include: Procter & Gamble; the Ford Taurus team; IBM credit; and Dodge's Neon design team. As a result of breaking down divisions between different departments, such as engineering and manufacturing, and putting product development in "platform teams," the Neon team took its car from conception to delivery in thirty-one months. A record previously unheard of in automobile manufacturing. All of these organizations have significantly reduced the amount of time it takes to move products to market as a result of organizing around small, functional teams tasked with getting the work done.

Realistically, is it possible to move from the bureaucratic design to interconnected teams overnight? No! But if you keep this design in mind and work to design your organizations in this way as much as possible, you will significantly increase organizational learning and creativity.

At the very least, work to eliminate the "silo mentality" that the bureaucratic organization promotes. Instead, organize around tasks that need to be accomplished and the expertise of the people you have hired to complete those tasks.

TEAMING UP TO ACHIEVE RESULTS

Robb LaBranche and Greg McGlone are effective leaders who have worked on developing a creative, participative work environment for several years now. The two are committed employees of Sherritt International and Viridian Inc.—formerly Sherritt Inc., a diversified public company based in Alberta, Canada, with 1700 employees and $1.5 billion in assets.

The department Greg worked in set an ambitious target of saving $5 million in five years through a major work redesign. Four years into the project, they are achieving tremendous success—both financially and from a quality of life perspective—for the department and its employees.

Robb, the organizational development specialist, Greg, a business unit manager, and the department team-development contact launched the initiative by identifying team-based problem-solving as a crucial component of the change process. The department's goal was to move from functional groups to cross-functional teams.

Shortly after the department work redesign was implemented, Robb and the department's management team delivered department-wide training in the basics of problem-solving. Two years later, volunteer employees were trained as Creative Problem Solving facilitators. Finally, the entire department (about 100 people) received two days of CPS basic training.

As part of the department training, ten department opportunities were selected as work goals. Three of the opportunites chosen were:

1. The need for a more flexible work and vacation schedule.
2. The opportunity to expand involvement in decision making.
3. Exploring ways of balancing recognition and responsibility in people's jobs.

Participants also used CPS to work on issues regarding the annual plant shutdown and to plan and implement additional training programs.

So how did it turn out? Shortly after initiating the training, Greg's business unit ran into a major operational problem with a new line that produced fertilizer. The line was expected to produce thirty-five tons per hour, yet after two weeks, it produced no more than twenty-eight tons per hour. Greg commissioned three of the trained CPS facilitators to take on the challenge at a Monday morning meeting. Along with fifteen resource group members, they worked on the problem for two hours, then dedicated a five person team to work on the problem until 4:00 P.M. that Wednesday.

Within two days, the facility was up to the target of thirty-five tons per hour. Since implementing all of the solutions the team created, the facility now produces forty tons per hour. The product sells for $300 per ton, so it's easy to see how this solution paid for the training program in a relatively short time.

BOTTOM LINE IMPACT

Do you see now how organizational environment makes a dramatic difference on whether people will express their creativity or stifle it? The experience of Robb and Greg show that a positive organizational environment that nurtures creativity can have a direct impact on bottom-line profits.

And that, after all, is the name of the game.

ENVIRONMENTAL STIMULANTS TO CREATIVITY AND INNOVATION

Freedom (74 percent)
Freedom in deciding what to do or how to accomplish the task; a sense of control over one's own work and ideas.

Good Project Management (65 percent)
A manager who serves as a good role model is enthusiastic, has good communication skills, protects the project team from outside distractions and interference, matches tasks to workers' skills and interests, and sets a clear direction without managing too tightly.

Sufficient Resources (52 percent)
Access to necessary resources, including facilities, equipment, information, funds, and people.

Encouragement (47 percent)
Management enthusiasm for new ideas, creating an atmosphere free of threatening evaluation.

Various Organizational Characteristics (42 percent)
A mechanism for considering new ideas; a corporate climate marked by cooperation and collaboration across levels and divisions; an atmosphere where innovation is prized and failure is not fatal.

Recognition (35 percent)
A general sense that creative work will receive appropriate feedback, recognition, and reward.

Sufficient Time (33 percent)
Time to think creatively about the problem, to explore different perspectives rather than having to impose an already-determined approach.

Challenge (22 percent)
A sense of challenge arising from the intriguing nature of the problem itself or its importance to the organization.

Pressure (12 percent)
A sense of urgency that is internally generated from competition with outside organizations, or from a general desire to accomplish something important.

      Think about your organization. How many of Amabile's stimulants to creativity exist in your company? What can you do to develop more stimulants?

ENVIRONMENTAL OBSTACLES TO CREATIVITY AND INNOVATION

Constraint (48 percent)
Lack of freedom in deciding what to do or how to accomplish the task; lack of sense of control over one's own work and ideas.

Organizational Disinterest (39 percent)
A lack of organizational support, interest, or faith in a

project; a perceived apathy toward any accomplishments coming from the project.

Poor Project Management (37 percent)
Manager unable to set clear direction; manager with poor technical or communication skills; manager who controls too tightly or allows distractions and fragmentation of the team's efforts.

Evaluation (35 percent)
Inappropriate or inequitable evaluation and feedback systems; unrealistic expectations; an environment focused on criticism and external evaluation.

Insufficient Resources (33 percent)
A lack of appropriate facilities, equipment, materials, funds, or people.

Time Pressure (33 percent)
Insufficient time to think creatively about the problem; too great a workload within an unrealistic time frame; high frequency of "fire-fighting"

Overemphasis on the Status Quo (26 percent)
Reluctance of managers or coworkers to change their way of doing things; an unwillingness to take risks.

Competition (14 percent)
Threatening, win-lose interpersonal or inter-group competition.
    Think about your organization. How many of Amabile's obstacles to creativity exist in your company? What can you do to remove those obstacles?

FOURTEEN

Creating a Climate for Growth

*It is the role of the creative leader to provoke thinking in the
minds of her followers, not to stifle their thinking.*
HAL STEVENS

One of the best examples I've ever seen of top management
doing the innovation process right occurred when one of my
colleagues and I were helping an organization generate ideas
for new markets. The morning session had ended and the
leader of this division, who had been in the session, asked to
have lunch with us. Peter said he wanted to give us some
"feedback" on the morning. Now, usually when someone tells
us they want to give us feedback, we expect to hear all the
things we did wrong. Not this time. In a few quick minutes this
gentleman told us five or six things he thought were particularly effective about how we conducted the session.

We waited to hear the rest of the "feedback," all the
things we did wrong. Surprise! There wasn't any. Our client
simply finished his lunch, and we were done.

Was this boss a softy? Was he permanently fitted with
rose-colored glasses? Absolutely not. He was the first to confront the group when problems or misunderstandings
occurred. He also supported his people when they came up
with new ideas. By the way, this business unit was one of the
most profitable in the organization and had a reputation for
bringing new product ideas to market in record time.

This leader was modeling the behavior he wanted to see
in his people. He honestly supported new ideas and accomplishments. His continued presence throughout the session
sent a strong message to his people. It said, "This training is
important. I want to learn all that I can about this so that we
use it in the company."

Six years after I conducted this session, I was invited back to the corporation to present a company-wide program. At the break, Peter came up to me. He told me he had attended the session that day "just to brush up" on his creativity skills.

He also told me, as did others from various parts of the organization, that his division is still one of the most profitable strategic business units in the corporation. "You know," Peter said, "I heard a number of people asking you questions today about how they could get others in their divisions to use Creative Problem Solving on a regular basis, to make it a way of doing business. We thought that was important, too. I believe it is easier for me to make this a way of doing business because I lead this division. And I would really like to see the entire organization working this way. But instead of trying to mandate it from the top, we have decided to set an example. We want to provide an excellent example of what these methods can do, so that when people come to us and ask us why and how we are doing so well, we can tell them. We have decided to teach by example."

ORGANIZATIONAL ENVIRONMENT, CULTURE, AND CLIMATE

As Peter well knows, it is the leader who sets the tone for his organization. More than anyone else, he has the power to shape the environment of his organization-whether that environment nurtures creativity or crushes it. The climate of most organizations simply reflects the leader's attitudes and actions.

What is meant by "organizational culture"? Culture is the beliefs, traditions, and values of the people in an organization. Culture is long-standing, deeply-rooted, usually develops slowly, and is often very painful to change. It is the cause of the behaviors and events that take place in an organization.

Culture is often below the awareness of the people in the organization. When I have asked people in interviews to tell me about their organizational culture, a common response is, "Well, I can't quite explain it, but it is just the way we do things around here."

On the other hand, "climate" or "environment" is much more visible and more behavior-based. According to Goran

Ekvall, it is the attitudes, feelings, and behaviors which characterize life in an organization. Although climate is not identical to organizational culture, it can be regarded as a manifestation of culture in the visible and audible behavior patterns of the organizational members.

Climate influences organizational processes such as problem-solving, decision-making, communications, coordination, and controlling, as well as the psychological processes of learning, creating, motivation, and commitment.

So what is the climate for creativity in an organization? Can we measure it? If so, can we enhance it for optimum creative productivity? Could we also help leaders set the organizational climate that will grow their companies?

The answer to all of those questions is Yes, thanks to our friend Goran Ekvall and his work on the Climate for Creativity Questionnaire (CCQ), to which we were introduced in the last chapter. Here I'd like to give a few more specifics on the questionnaire in order to provide you with some powerful tools to gauge the effectiveness of your own organization.

MEASURING THE ENVIRONMENT FOR CREATIVITY

The Climate for Creativity Questionnaire grew out of a research program that began in Sweden during the 1980s on the organizational conditions that stimulate or hamper creativity and innovation[1] It is a fifty-item questionnaire that consists of ten dimensions of five items each. The item pool on which the questionnaire construction is based came from theory, field research, and consulting experiences in organizational psychology.

According to Ekvall, the CCQ is grounded in some basic construction principles. First, it is an organizational measure, not an individual one. The respondent is addressed as an observer of the life in the organization. She is asked to tell how people in the workplace usually behave. She is not to report about her own behavior nor communicate her personal feelings. This questionnaire is not a job satisfaction inventory. There is no "I" or "me" in the items. A consequence of this objective conception of climate is that the observer, the respondent, is requested to report on common *behavior*, not on common *opinions*. A typical item might be phrased, "It is common here for people to take initiatives of their own."

THE TEN FACTORS OF THE CCQ

One: Challenge
The emotional involvement of the members of the organization in its operations and goals. In a high-challenge climate people find great joy and meaning in their jobs, and as a result invest a great deal of energy in it. In a low challenge environment people feel alienated and indifferent. The common sentiment and attitude is apathy and lack of interest for the job and the organization.

Two: Freedom
The independence in behavior exerted by the people in the organization. In a climate with a good amount of freedom, people talk and work with each other to give and receive information and discuss problems and alternatives. They plan and take initiatives of different kinds and they make decisions. A low freedom environment produces people who are passive, fixated by the rules of the organization, and careful to stay inside its established boundaries.

Three: Idea Support
The ways new ideas are treated. In a supportive climate, ideas and suggestions are received in an attentive and positive way by bosses and coworkers. People listen to each other and encourage initiatives. Possibilities for trying out new ideas are created. The atmosphere is constructive and positive. When idea support is low, "no" is the prevailing response. Every suggestion is immediately rebuffed by a counterargument. Raising obstacles to change and finding fault in ideas is the usual way of responding to ideas.

Four: Trust/Openness
The emotional safety in relationships. When there is a strong level of trust, everyone in the organization feels comfortable in putting ideas and opinions forward. Initiatives can be taken without fear of reprisals and ridicule in case of failure. Communication is open and straightforward. When trust is

missing, people are suspicious of each other and can expect to pay a high cost for their mistakes. People are also afraid of being exploited and robbed of their good ideas.

Five: Dynamism/Liveliness
The eventfulness of life in the organization. In the highly dynamic organization, new things are happening all the time. There are a variety of ways of thinking about and handling issues. People in these organizations describe a kind of psychological turbulence as "full speed," "go," "breakneck," and "maelstrom."

The opposite situation could be compared to a slow "jog" with no surprises. There are no new projects, no different plans. Everything goes its usual, customary, expected way.

Six: Playfulness/Humor
The spontaneity and ease displayed in an organization, characterized by a relaxed atmosphere with jokes and laughter. The opposite climate reeks of gravity and seriousness, with a stiff, gloomy, and cumbrous atmosphere. Jokes and laughter are regarded as improper.

Seven: Debates
The interaction and clashes between viewpoints, ideas, and differing experiences and knowledge. In a debating organization, many voices are heard and people are eager to put forward their ideas. When debate is missing, people follow authoritarian patterns without questioning. Debates can be characterized by "collisions between ideas" as opposed to collisions between people.

Eight: Conflicts
The presence of personal and emotional tensions (in contrast with idea tensions) in the organization. When the level of conflict is high, groups and individuals hate each other and the climate can be characterized by "warfare." Plots and traps are usual elements in the life of the organization. Gossip and slander are common. Conflicts are collisions between people as opposed to collisions between ideas.

In the opposite case, people behave in a more mature

manner; they demonstrate psychological insight and control of impulses. This is the only "negative dimension" in the Climate for Creativity Questionnaire; that is, more of this dimension is detrimental to an environment that nurtures creativity.

Nine: Risk-Taking

The tolerance for uncertainty in an organization. In a high risk-taking organization, decisions and actions are prompt and rapid. New opportunities are seized and taking action is preferred to detailed investigation and analysis. In a risk-avoiding climate, people exhibit a cautious, hesitant mentality. They try to be on the "safe side" and often decide "to sleep on the matter." They set up committees and cover themselves in many ways before making a decision.

Ten: Idea Time

The amount of time people can use (and do use) for developing new ideas. In the high idea-time organization, the possibilities exist to discuss and test impulses and fresh suggestions that are not planned or included in the task assignment. In the opposite environment, every minute is booked and specified. Time pressure makes it impossible to think outside the day-to-day, structured activities and planned routines.

CAN A CREATIVE ENVIRONMENT MAKE A DIFFERENCE?
If the environment for creativity is important and improves results, then it follows that organizations identified as innovative (in terms of products, services, methods, policies, etc.) should differ in climate from deliberately conservative or unintentionally outdistanced organizations. Studies with the CCQ support this conclusion.

The following study presents a comparison between a group of ten innovative and a group of five stagnated organizations.[2] The organizations in this study are small companies (100 to 200 employees) or an independent division of a larger corporation. "Innovative" refers to product innovations. The ten innovative organizations have been successful in developing new, profitable products that have done well in the marketplace.

The five stagnated organizations needed to upgrade their

product programs but either had not tried or had tried with little or no results. Stagnated organizations, despite an obvious need to change, had not managed to make the necessary adjustments. All employees in the representative sample answered the CCQ. The dots in the figure on page 210 represent the average scores for the organizations in the two groups.

For there to be a significant difference on the dimensions, a difference of .3 is required. For those with a statistical bent, these differences are significant at the .05 level or better on all ten climate dimensions. That means there is a 95 percent chance that these ratings are not due to chance.

I hope you're not tired of studies, because I'd like to introduce you briefly to yet another one. The chart on page 211 shows how three subsidiaries of a large, multi-national corporation fared on the CCQ.[3] One subsidiary was Swedish, one German, and one Spanish. The study was part of a corporate-wide program for promoting innovation. All levels of employees were represented in the samples—managers, white-collar workers, and blue-collar workers.

The top-management group of the corporation's Research and Development division ranked the three companies regarding their innovative achievements. All of the raters agreed that the German division was the most innovative, the Swedish division was the next most innovative and the Spanish division ranked last. Objective indications of innovation—such as number of patents and the amount of activity in each division's suggestion programs—validated the rankings.

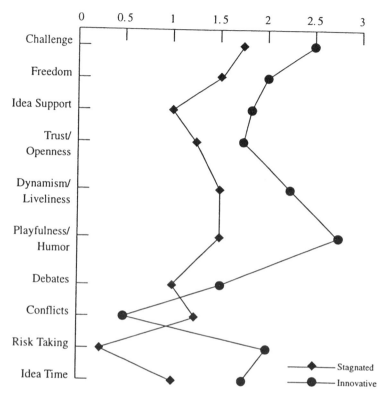

According to Ekvall, several of the dimensions of the CCQ are climate aspects that affect more than creativity and innovation.[4] Challenge, Freedom, Trust, Playfulness, and low Conflicts positively influence productivity, quality, and well-being, in addition to innovation.

Optimal levels on these dimensions may vary. There can be too much Playfulness in some contexts, which might decrease quality; or too much Freedom may have a negative effect on productivity.

Some of the other CCQ-dimensions are more specifically related to creativity and innovation. These are: Idea-support, Debates, Risk-taking and Idea time. In all studies conducted thus far, a higher rating on the Risk-taking dimension is the greatest differentiating factor between innovative and stagnated organizations. High risk-taking, however important for innovation, is not appropriate in a hospital operating room or in an airplane cockpit.

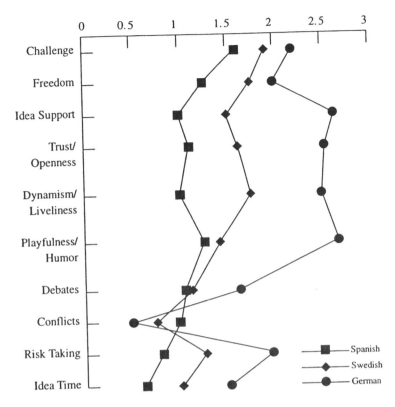

Risk-taking, Dynamism, Freedom, and Debates seem to be the climate dimensions that make the crucial difference between the creative climate that supports radical innovation and the one that focuses only on incremental improvement.

Whew! Enough statistics? Are you convinced? If you still need some convincing (or if you are interested in more information on using the Climate for Creativity Questionnaire), please contact me and I will be happy to provide you with information on how you can use a version of this instrument in your organization. The address is given on page 226.

CAN IT WORK FOR YOU?
The question is, can the CCQ work in your organization? And if so, how can you use the information presented in the last two chapters to change the environment in your organization? How can you as a leader use the dimensions of the CCQ to make your organization a more innovative, productive, and

better place to work?

One way is to formally take the CCQ, have it administered to all your employees, and then be debriefed by a professional in the creativity field. Another way is to take a few moments to answer the following ten questions and see how you would rate your organization on the dimensions on the CCQ.

(Let me remind you, the following is not the CCQ. The CCQ has five times as many questions as you're about to answer. But these ten questions can give you some idea of what the strengths of your organization might be and where some of its weaknesses might be.)

Ask the following questions of your direct reports, of your executive team, and of your key managers. Consider using them with other people in your organization who might provide some enlightening input as to how your organization treats ideas and how it uses those ideas for creative and innovative productivity. Score your answers on a three-point scale: 1 = poor; 2 = fair; 3 = good. Ready? Let's go!

1. *Challenge.* The people in this organization really care about their work and take pride and ownership in what they do.
2. *Freedom.* People in this organization are free to try new ways to get their work done.
3. *Idea support.* People listen to each other in this organization and encourage each other's ideas.
4. *Trust and openness.* People in this organization feel comfortable discussing their ideas with others.
5. *Dynamism and liveliness.* There's a great deal going on in this organization. It's an exciting place to work.
6. *Playfulness and humor.* It's common here to see people joking good naturedly, laughing, and enjoying their work.
7. *Debates.* It's common to see people discussing each other's ideas and ways of accomplishing things in this organization.
8. *Conflicts.* People generally don't talk negatively behind each other's back, and when conflicts arise, they are quickly resolved.

9. *Risk taking.* People in this organization are generally not penalized for failure. They can take risks on new initiatives and put those ideas into action.
10. *Idea time.* There is ample time to discuss, develop, and initiate new ideas in this organization. It is common to have regular sessions where employees meet to discuss better ways of doing business.

After you've taken this abbreviated questionnaire, review your answers. It's highly unlikely you scored a three on each one. If you did, I'm pretty sure you were looking through rose-colored glasses. It's better to use these questions as discussion starters with others in your organization. The questions can also serve as a guide to using appropriate parts of this book that can help you to improve the dimensions of your organization that are weak.

For example, if you found that your organization rated low on Challenge, do you allow your employees to do their job better? Do you set the direction and get out of their way? If not, take a look at chapters 1, 2, and 10.

If you rated low on Freedom, review chapters 5, 10, and 11.

Rated low on Idea Support? Then take a look at chapters 6, 7, 8, 9, and 10.

If you need help with Trust and Openness, review chapters 5, 6, 9, and 13.

Is Dynamism and Liveliness the problem? Then take a look at chapters 5 and 6. They will give you some tools to help the organization *move.*

Does your organization lack Playfulness and Humor? Then see the section on humor in chapter 2 and review chapter 12.

If you struggle with Debates, reread chapters 3, 4, 7, and 8. Phrasing problems in a way they can be solved and using the PPC technique to evaluate ideas will give you a structure with which to conduct effective debates, debates that move issues forward and create action.

If you rated high on Conflicts, see chapters 2, 3, and 9.

Do you rate low on Risk-Taking? Then refer back to chapters 5, 7, 11, and 12.

Does your company lack Idea Time? Look in chapters 5, 9, and 10 for ways to change. It's important to remember that if you want creativity to flourish in your organization, you need to create the space for it—so also take another look at chapters 1 and 2.

BLUE SKY THAT WORKS

How do you get people intrinsically motivated in your organization to produce creatively? Answer: Have people discover what they're good at doing and enjoy doing, let them do it, and praise and recognize them for it. I realize that might seem like a blue sky approach to an organization, but it is absolutely possible.

In his book, *Artful Work: Awakening Joy, Meaning and Commitment in the Workplace,* Dick Richards relates the following story of organizational redesign based on intrinsic motivation. He calls it "The spaghetti method of organizational redesign."

Susan was the director of a human service agency in trouble. Her organization provided both medical and counseling services. The agency's staff included six nurses, six counselors, three records assistants, and two receptionists. But Susan's funding was shrinking.

She believed her most valued employees were those who helped the agency's clients to grow in their personal lives. She also believed that those employees who most helped clients grow were those who were themselves growing and who most enjoyed their work. She knew she could not afford to keep those valued employees for long. If they were growing, they would also want increasingly more challenging opportunities. The situation is similar to corporations that now recognize they can no longer offer "lifetime employment."

Susan said, "I'd be suspicious of anyone who wanted to be here for more than four or five years. If they did, they wouldn't be growing. If they weren't growing, how could they help anyone else grow? They would stop enjoying themselves and their work would suffer because I couldn't provide the challenges or bribe them to stay by offering more money, even if I wanted to." continued on page 215

continued from page 214

She relinquished the idea that her agency could provide "long-term employment." She focused instead on "long-term employability" for her people. First, she asked each employee to create a statement that included answers to these questions:

- What are your personal long-term goals?
- How does your employment here contribute to your goals?
- What might you do differently here so that you would enjoy your work and contribute more significantly to your goals?
- What kind of training do you need in order to do what you might do differently here?
- How does what you might do differently contribute to the agency's mission and meet our clients' needs?

Susan met with each person to discuss his or her statements. She then held a meeting of all employees. She began by saying, "As of this moment there are no jobs here, but all of you are employed here. In this meeting we will reinvent everybody's job. As we do this we will ensure that we are faithful to the agency's mission, our clients' needs, and our own individual goals. Each of us will declare what work would give us the most enjoyment and growth. We will describe how the changes we want to make in our own work will benefit our clients and how those changes fit our mission." She also committed to provide training, within the limits of her resources. The group created lists on large paper of what they needed to do to fulfill the agency's mission, what they now did, what they wanted to do, and what they felt their clients needed. They cut the lists into strips, one item per strip.

Then they sat in a circle surrounding a pile of paper strips. Someone remarked that the pile looked like some weird kind of spaghetti. Susan said, "Let us begin picking up the strips. Pick up the strips you want."

Thus was Susan's agency redesigned-with concern for joy and growth, clients' needs, empowered choice, and organizational mission. One counselor became a licensed psychologist. A records assistant trained to become a counselor.

continued from page 216

continued from page 215

A nurse learned supervision. Susan did research about the effects of her approach on the agency's clients. Her research confirmed the effectiveness of the approach.[8]

The application for you? Talk to your people and find out what motivates them. What do they like to do? What are they good at? How would they like to be recognized and rewarded? You might be pleasantly surprised with what you discover.

SUGGESTIONS FROM THE FRONT LINES

Tools like Ekvall's CCQ can give companies specific help in fine-tuning their organizations in order to encourage innovation and creativity. But in some ways, there's no advice better than that which comes from the front lines. Therefore, let's consider a few suggestions from those who are even now implementing ideas designed to create a more favorable environment for creativity.

One: Achieve Early Success

When Janet DiClaudio was Director of Medical Records at Candler Hospital in Savannah, Georgia, she gave the following suggestions for applying creativity skills. "I tell my staff that they are to evaluate nothing, don't worry about the money, don't worry about anything, that's my job."

Janet encourages her staff to make as many suggestions as possible, and she will do her best to find the money to implement the idea. According to Janet, "If I don't have the money or if we can't do it, I'll let my people know."

Janet also lets her staff decide what problems they are having that prevent them from doing their job well, problems they would like to get fixed. Very early in the process of change, she encouraged her staff to select a problem they could easily fix so they would see immediate success and want to continue to use the creative process skills. It is crucial in any sort of change program that employees see some results early to create positive, self-sustaining momentum.

Two: When You Start the Process, Have a Strong Facilitator

Peter Pellegrino of EDS emphasized the importance of a strong facilitator in conducting Creative Problem Solving sessions properly. "One of the other things that worked for us at EDS was the way the Creative Problem Solving sessions were conducted. It is important during a brainstorming session to observe those ground rules of not judging ideas and getting a free flow of information. When these sessions are facilitated properly, so people feel that they're really allowed to stretch and think out of the box, then they are convinced of the value of this process.

"If, however, the Creative Problem Solving sessions are not facilitated properly, people get turned off very quickly. If you go through the ground rules and say freewheeling is allowed and think out of the box and then the facilitator allows judgment to be passed, that turns people off very quickly."

Peter emphasized, "With a new group it's easy to get lost, it's easy not to have things go the way you would want them to go. A strong facilitator is essential until everybody gets used to using the Creative Problem Solving process."[5]

Three: Train Top Management First

In attempting to apply creativity skills, it is crucial that the top management is trained first. They should also be trained the most. This involvement is important because when top management is trained, they are then in a position to teach their subordinates, coach the application, and reinforce the use of creativity skills.

As a supervisor or as a manager, it's important that you walk the talk and that you model the behavior you are trying to create in the organization. If creativity is important to you then you have to be creative. You need to struggle with the crazy ideas and show your people that it is acceptable for you and them not to have the "correct" answer all the time. In this way you encourage your staff to experiment with their novel ideas. Your people are watching your lead, and whatever your lead is, they will follow it. By not having all the ideas—all the time—for all the situations, you create a sense of purpose and a need for others to develop their abilities.

Peter Pellegrino of EDS emphasized the importance of upper management support when implementing any change process. "From the top, there needs to be a climate created where people feel that what they come up with is going to be accepted and implemented," he said. "They need to have a little faith that there is going to be buy-in from the top to use Creative Problem Solving. We were fortunate with our process in that we had second level managers who were always in our corner, who were always taking what we did and sharing it with their peers, defending it with their peers, willing to really go to the mat for us. From my perspective, we wouldn't have gotten anywhere if we didn't have that support."[6]

Four: Get Skeptics to Participate First

As in any change effort, there are going to be skeptics. So it is important to get those skeptics involved right up front. Get them involved generating problem statements and ideas for solving those problems. Make sure that they see those ideas implemented. Once you get that hard-to-convince group involved and they see the power of this process and they see it work, the rest of the organization tends to follow very quickly.

"I can't stress enough the fact that the real buy-in for our group here came from actually seeing ideas generated and then implemented," Peter Pellegrino said. "I don't know if that's unique to this culture, but that's what finally made people realize that this was something that they could work with, that they could live with, and part of their daily job included the fact that they were able to generate ideas and then actually see them implemented."

Five: Understand That Both Union and Management Benefit

Nathan Bliss, United Auto Workers Education and Problem Solving Training Coordinator at General Motors Saginaw Division Forge Plant, emphasized that unions can assist in implementing creativity or any sort of change program. He calls the union and management relationship "athletic." According to Nathan, "If the unions are permitted buy-in and have an active role to play, it's sort of athletic in nature. Most people who play tennis, racquet-ball, or golf, usually go with a friend. There are days when you're about not to go, and your buddy calls you up and says, 'Let's go hit nine.' So you go along and you're always happy that you did. It's a symbiotic relationship?"

HOW TO EFFECT THE ENVIRONMENT FOR CREATIVITY

While pursuing my doctorate, I became very interested in the effects of Creative Problem Solving training on the communication behaviors that occur in small groups. In organizations, it is in the small group where new ideas are born and, in many cases, where new ideas die. This is particularly true as we structure our organizations in an information age configuration. In this study we used twenty groups of students of five members each who were trained in Creative Problem Solving and compared them with twenty five-member groups who were not trained in Creative Problem Solving.

We took the students to the television studio on our campus, and gave them an actual business problem to solve. As shown in the chart below, when we analyzed the videotapes we found that the groups that were trained in Creative Problem Solving participated significantly more.

They criticized ideas significantly less. They supported ideas significantly more. They laughed significantly more. And bottom line, did they generate more ideas? Yes. Over two to one.

Effects of Creative Problem Solving Training on Communication Behaviors in Small Groups

	Untrained	Trained
Total Responses	26	39
Verbal Criticism	2.2	0.9
Verbal Support	1.4	3.7
Laughter	2.1	6.0
Smiles	2.6	6.7
Ideas Generated	13	27

There are times when the union wants to do something and management says, "We don't want it." But for the sake of the relationship and the environment, management supports the idea. There are also times when management really gets excited about something and says, ‛"Hey, let's do this!" Then the union sometimes says, "Okay, if that's really what you want, we will support you.'

When a change initiative is beginning and union and management support one another, there is an opportunity to do a great deal more than could otherwise have been achieved. Why? Because the environment is set for action.

Six: Be Patient with the Process of Change

As Peter Pellegrino of EDS emphasized, "Be patient at the onset when introducing all of this change to the organization. Work on something small at first to get people used to the process. For example, don't try to solve world hunger right away and don't try to apply Creative Problem Solving to a huge laundry list of problems until everybody is comfortable with what they're doing. We found that it tends to grow on its own when you start small and let things come as they may"[7]

Peter uses this analogy when he talks about change in the organization:

> It's a like a road. We didn't start the first day with a luxurious, six-lane highway with rest stops and all the nice stuff. We started with a very simple path and very slowly built up to where we are. We didn't try to go from a dirt road to a six-lane highway. We made logical steps. We took steps that we could accomplish. In a short time we built off short-term goals, all the while having our long-term vision in mind. We were careful to build off short-term goals so that we were able to enjoy some sort of success. That helped to keep our morale up and to keep our vision going.
>
> Make sure that you set short-term goals and that you have a long-range direction. Then reward short-term goals and accomplishments to keep people interested and motivated.

Seven: Combine Creative Problem Solving with Complementary Skills

It helps to apply Creative Problem Solving in organizational settings by combining these methods with complementary skills. Effective people rarely use narrow skills; they typically use broad skill sets. Creativity skills, teamwork, and group management skills, combined with a focus on a specific purpose, will lead to success. A closer look at these skills reveals that each is inherently dependent upon the other; only in that way can they be applied effectively. This is one reason why narrow, singular skill development has limited results. Unfortunately, we typically train people in narrow skill areas.

According to Nathan Bliss, before implementing Creative Problem Solving and additional analytical techniques, out of every 100 parts that were being sent to Saturn Gear, seventeen would be sent back to the plant as rejects. As a result of combining Creative Problem Solving with additional analytical methods, in the three months following the implementation of these techniques, 859,000 pieces were sent to Saturn Gear- and only six were returned as defects. For all practical purposes, this is zero defect.

MAZDA MOTOR MANUFACTURING, USA CORPORATION

In the summer of 1986, the phone rang in my office in Buffalo, New York. It was Ken Kumiega. Ken had recently been hired as the director of training and development for Mazda Motor Manufacturing, USA. As the sixth person of the launch team hired in this new organization, it was Ken's job to develop the type of work environment and train the anticipated 3,500 people that Mazda would hire to build the MX-6, the Ford Probe, and the Mazda 626. This plant in Flatrock, Michigan, was Mazda's first auto manufacturing enterprise in the United States. As such, the Japanese management had some concerns and plenty of excitement about launching the operation.

Mazda was attempting to create a new culture for building cars. They intended to do this through extensive training and development, an organizational system based on teams, and through innovative screening and hiring practices. The people hired to build the cars at this plant came from three areas: (1) Individuals who had previous experience in the automobile manufacturing industry; (2) people who had unrelated experience in the industry (i.e., individuals in leasing or car sales); and (3) people who had no experience in the industry. It would not be uncommon, then, for someone who was a house-wife several months before to be hired to run a state-of-the-art automatic transfer steel stamping press.

Every one of the 3,500 people to be hired in the plant were to be trained in a number of programs. Those programs consisted of quality tools, continuous improvement, how to work effectively in teams, and Creative Problem Solving, along with job-specific technical training.

My role was to develop a one-day training program in Creative Problem Solving that I would deliver to the members of the training staff. They, in turn, would train all the new hires that would come into the plant.

Ken, with a budget of $42 million, spent close to $37 million to train members and prepare the organization to be a world leader in automobile manufacturing. As such, he was very interested in results. So what did he get for his money?

The first sale model of the 1988 626LX came off the line at 9:01 A.M. on September 1, 1987-right on schedule. By the way, this was the first sale model. Mazda already had pro-duced 300 "engineering mules" and pre-production cars to test the work and manufacturing systems and the skills of mem-bers. Some of these cars would be given to staff members to drive (and drive hard) to further evaluate the product design.

Later, when I interviewed Ken about his work at Mazda and asked him to relate it to the use of creativity, he gave me what is today Kumiega's model for "creative output" (which is what much of this book is based on): "Creativity Skills + Environment + Application = Creative Output."

Ken's comments are used with his permission:

> In our work at Mazda Motor Manufacturing, USA, we prepared our members by giving them training in "cre-ativity skills," team-work skills, and constant process improvement methodologies. We also addressed the "environment" to ensure that support systems promoted these methods and provided encouragement and rein-forcement. Finally, we addressed the "application" of

these skills through a clear focus and constancy of purpose. This combined approach helped us to create a new work culture that nurtured the generation of ideas and innovation.

When we evaluated the effects of this approach, we found that as "creative output" people came up to speed faster in terms of meeting productivity and quality levels by days, not simply by minutes. Also, members' contributions in identifying improvement needs and solutions through suggestions was key in establishing an overall approach to continuous quality improvement. When you look at a company such as Mazda that values improvements in terms of minutes and seconds—and when the organization was able to reach quality and productivity target levels in *fewer days*—these results are significant.

That's what consciously creating a creativity-friendly environment did for Mazda. And there's no reason it can't do the same for you. But you've got to make the choice. It really is up to you.

EPILOGUE
The Final Word — and an Invitation

———❖———

What it all comes down to, leader, is that if you want your organization to change, if you want to transform your organization to one that fosters the creativity of its people, you have to change. You have to become creative.

Sorry, no management system, training program, workshop, seminar, book or videotape can change your organization for you. All of them can help give some tools—but you must make the commitment to change. *You* must make the commitment to creativity.

Nevertheless, you are not alone and you are not without proven tools that work. Leaders of all kinds of organizations across the world are applying Creative Problem Solving to create results, helping the people in their organizations to nurture their creativity. And the result is nearly always advancement, profitability, and success for the company.

Several years ago, I took a personal growth seminar, where I was asked to examine the things in my life to which I was committed. As a result of that program, my commitment to others is this: "To help you apply your creativity in your world to create results." To honor that commitment I deliver speeches, conduct workshops, write books, produce audio and videotapes, consult with leaders, and train people to facilitate Creative Problem Solving in their organizations. I also publish a newsletter, *Innovation Espresso*. The newsletter is free and is designed to keep you up-to-date on some of the latest work in the field of creativity and innovation. It is also a great reminder of some of the principles discussed in this book.

If you are interested in receiving information on programs in Creative Problem Solving that my organization delivers, or if you want to receive *Innovation Espresso,* please contact me at:

Innovation Resources, Inc.
P.O. Box 615
Williamsville, NY 14231-0615
(716) 631-3564
www.RogerFirestien.com

Another crucial part of creativity is networking. If you want to contact any of the people interviewed in this book, reach me at the address above and I will be happy to get you their most recent contact information. In that way, you can correspond with them directly.
Onward and upward!

Notes

One: The Key to Your Company's Success
1. Goran Ekvall, *Organizational Climate for Creativity and Innovation. European Journal of Work and Organizational Psychology,* vol. 5, no. 1 (1996), pp. 105-123.
2. Jon Berry and Edward Ogiba, "It's Your Boss," *Brandweek* magazine, vol. 27, no. 39, 19 October 1992, pp. 18-25.
3. "1992 Innovation Survey: Report on New Products," Group EFO Limited.
4. Berry and Ogiba, *Brandweek,* p. 18.
5. S. S. Gryskiewicz, "Predictable Creativity," in S. G. Isaken, ed., *Frontiers of Creativity Research: Beyond the Basics* (Buffalo, N.Y.: Bearly Limited, 1987), pp. 305-313.
6. Gene Koretz, "Sweet Carrots, Big Gains: Workers Say Incentives Work," *Business Week,* 10 July 1995, p. 24.
7. Carol Anderson, from a personal conversation, January 1996. Used by permission.
8. Abraham Maslow, *Creativity in Self-Actualizing People,* in H. H. Anderson, ed., *Creativity and Its Cultivation* (New York: Harper & Row, 1959), no page.
9. Source unknown.

Two: Fly the Fruitful Skies
1. John Gardner, *On Leadership* (New York: The Free Press, 1990), p. 155.
2. Donna Hamlin, Hamlin & Harkin Associates, from personal correspondence, 1989. Used by permission.
3. R V. Farace, P. R. Monge, and H. M. Russell, *Communicating and Organizing* (Redding, Mass.: Addison-Wesley, 1977), pp. 177-203.
4. Perry W. Buffington, from personal communication, December 1995. Used by permission.
5. Joan Borysenko, *Minding the Body, Mending the Mind* (New York: Bantam Books, 1987), pp. 25-26.
6. Anthony Storr, *Solitude: A Return to the Self* (New York: Ballentine Books, 1988), p. 36.
7. George Kneller, *The Art and Science of Creativity* (New York: Holt, Rinehart and Winston, 1965), no page.
8. Survey by Rita Dunn, Ken Dunn, and G. E. Price, *Learning Style Inventory: Productivity Environmental Preference Survey* (Lawrence, Kans.: Price Systems Inc., 1993).
9. R. S. Dunn, J. S. Krimsky, J. B. Murray, and P. J. Quinn, "Light Up Their Lives: A Review of Research on the Effects of Lighting on Children's Achievement and Behaviors," *Reading-Teacher,* vol. 38, no. 9, May 1985, pp. 863-869.
10. James Adams, *Conceptual Blockbusting: A Guide to Better Ideas* (New York: Addison-Wesley Publishing Co., Inc., 1986), p. 66.
11. Joel Goodman, from a personal conversation, January 1996. Used by permission.
12. Brian Tracy, "Psychology of Achievement: Six Keys to Personal Power," cassette recording (Chicago, Ill.: Nightingale-Conant Co., 1984).
13. E. Paul Torrance, "The Importance of Falling in Love with Something," *The Creative Child and Adult Quarterly,* vol. 8, no. 2 (1983), pp. 72-78.

14. Torrance, pp. 72-78.
15. Torrance, pp. 72-78.

Three: Phrase Problems in a Way They Can Be Solved

1. S. J. Parnes, R. B. Noller, A. M. Biondi, *Guide to Creative Action* (New York: Scribners, 1977), p. 47.
2. Michael Michalko, *Thinkertoys* (Berkeley, Calif.: Ten Speed Press, 1991), p. 31.
3. Peter Pellegrino, from a personal conversation, December 1995. Used by permission.
4. Pellegrino.
5. Pellegrino.

Five: Defer Judgment and Generate Many Ideas

1. Alex Osborn, *Applied Imagination* (New York: Charles Scribner's Sons, 1953), p. 124.
2. Osborn, pp. 128-129.
3. Friedrich Schiller, quoted by Osborn, p. 127.
4. Robert Fulghum, *It Was On Fire When I Lay Down On It* (New York: Random House, 1988), p. 181.
5. Robert Eckert, from a personal conversation, November 1995. Used by permission.
6. Roger L. Firestien, "Effects of Creative Problem Solving on Communication Behaviors in Small Groups," *Small Group Research*, vol. 21, no. 4 (1990).
7. "U.S./Japan Suggestion-system Report: Bigger Ain't Better; More is Merrier," *Total Employee Involvement Newsletter* (Productivity Inc.), February 1993, p. 1.
8. "U.S./Japan."
9. "U.S./Japan."
10. "U.S./Japan."
11. Masaaki Imai, "The Key to Japan's Competitive Success," *Kaizen* (New York: McGraw Hill, 1986), no page.
12. Jeff Harris, from a personal conversation, January 1996. Used by permission.
13. Harris.
14. Harris.

Six: How to Conduct an Idea Generating Session

1. Nathan Bliss, *Unleashing the Power of Creativity*, video, Roger L. Firestien, producer (Buffalo, N.Y.: Kinetic, Inc., 1994).
2. Adapted from a form developed by the Center for Creative Leadership. See: B. Johannson, *Kreativatat and Marketing* (Switzerland: H. Kern AG, 1978). Further adapted by Scott G. Isaksen (1989), Blair J. Miller (1995), and Roger L. Firestien (1995).

Seven: Evaluate Ideas Positively

1. Arthur Gordon, "How Wonderful You Are: The Gift of Encouragement Can Inspire Greatness," *Possibilities*, July-August 1994, pp. 23-25.
2. Scott G. Isaksen, K. Brian Dorval, and Donald J. Treffinger, *Creative Approaches to Problem Solving* (Dubuque, Iowa: Kendall/Hunt, 1994), pp. 48-50.
3. The PPC was originally developed in the early 1980s by Diane Foucar-Szocki, Bill Shepard and Roger Firestien.

Eight: The Power of the PPC
1. E. M. Rogers, *Diffusion of Innovation, Third Edition* (New York: The Free Press, 1983).

Nine: Praise and Recognize Ideas
1. W. E. Brown, "Praise-Criticism Ratio: Do Teachers Take Advantages of It?" *Behaviorally Speaking,* May 1972, p. 11. This same study asked teachers to list the ways they tried to change student behaviors, then to group these behavior change methods into categories. Seven categories emerged, including: pain; fear and anxiety; frustration; humiliation and embarrassment; boredom; physical discomfort; positive comments.
2. Brown, p. 11.
3. Peter Grazer, *El Network,* Bi-monthly newsletter, September-October 1995, p. 1.
4. Robert Eckert, from a personal conversation, November 1995. Used by permission.
5. Daniel Goleman, *Emotional Intelligence: Why It Can Matter More Than IQ* (New York: Bantam, 1995), pp. 27-28.
6. Goleman, p. 151.
7. Goleman, p. 153.

Ten: Tootsie Rolls, Animal Crackers, and Other Odd Roads to Prosperity
1. Thomas J. Peters and Robert H. Waterman, *In Search of Excellence* (New York: Harper & Row, 1982), p. 54.
2. Peters and Waterman, pp. 57-58.
3. Peters and Waterman, p. 68.
4. Peters and Waterman, p. 70.
5. Peters and Waterman, pp. 70-71.
6. Teresa Amabile, "The Personality of Creativity," *Brandeis Review,* 1985 vol. 5,
no. 1, pp. 5-8.
7. Amabile, p. 7.
8. Albert Einstein, quoted by Amabile, p. 6.
9. Arthur Schawlow, quoted by Amabile, p. 6.
10. George Leonard, *Mastery* (New York: Penguin Group, 1991), pp. 57-58.
1 I. Leonard, p. 124.
12. Janet DiClaudio, "Praise, Praise and More Praise: Designing a Creative Environment in a Health Care Setting," *Leadership and Organization Development Journal,* Manchester School of Business, vol. 12, no. 4, pp. 28-31.
13. DiClaudio, p. 29.
14. DiClaudio, p. 30.
15. DiClaudio, p. 30.
16. James Charlton and Lisbeth Mark, *The Writer's Home Companion: Anecdotes, Comforts, Recollections and Other Amusements for Every Writer, Editor and Reader* (New York: Penguin Books, 1989), p. 93.
17. Alice Cuneo, "Diverse by Design," *Business Week,* October 1992, p. 72.

Eleven: Make Mistakes-and Learn from Them
1. Joel Achenbach, "When Genius Bombs," *Washington Post,* 16 April 1995, pp. G-1 to G-6.
2. Achenbach, p. G-6.
3. Dean Keith Simonton, *Greatness: Who Makes History and Why* (New York:

Guilford, 1994).
4. Story paraphrased from S. R. Grossman, B. E. Rodgers, and B. R. Moore, *Innovation, Inc.: Unlocking Creativity in the Workplace* (Plano, Tex.: Wordwear Publishing, Inc., 1988), pp. 79-81.
5. Leon Botstein, quoted by Achenbach, p. G-7.
6. John Gardner, *On Leadership* (New York: The Free Press, 1990), p. 135.
7. James Michener, quoted by Gardner, p. 135.
8. Dave Meier, from personal communication, October 1995. Used by permission.
9. Burt Rutan, quoted by Michael Maren and Duncan Maxwell Anderson, "Great Comebacks," *Success,* August 1989,   pp. 24-33.

Twelve: Trial and Error, or Trial and Learn?

1. J. C. Crimmons, producer, and M. Jackson, director, "Trial and Error," *Search for Solutions,* film (New York: Phillips Petroleum Co., 1979).
2. Crimmons and Jackson, "Context," *Search for Solutions.*
3. Melanie Brown, *Attaining Personal Greatness* (New York: William Morrow, 1987), pp. 78, 82.
4. Michael Warshaw, "Never Say Die," *Success,* August 1996, p. 35.
5. Warshaw, p. 35.
6. Warshaw, p. 37.
7. Warshaw, p. 37.
8. Quoted in "To Illustrate," *Leadership,* Winter 1983, vol. 4, no. 1, p. 83.
9. Crimmons and Jackson, "Trial and Error," *Search for Solutions.*
10. D. Berg, "Unleashing Energy and Enthusiasm," *ADVANCE for Administrators in Radiology,"* August 1995.

Thirteen: You Set the Environment

1. Goran Ekvall, *Organizational Climate for Creativity and Innovation, European Journal of Work and Organizational Psychology,* dental clinic study, vol. 5, no. I (1996), pp. 105-123.
2. Ekvall, pp. 105-123.
3. Ekvall, pp. 105-123.
4. Dave Meier, from personal correspondence, October 1995. Used by permission.
5. Teresa Amabile, "Assessing the Work Environment for Creativity: Promises and Pitfalls," keynote address at the Conference for Creativity and Change, Buffalo, New York, October 1995, pp. 7-8.

Fourteen: Creating a Climate for Growth

1. Adapted from Goran Ekvall, "Organizational Climate for Creativity and Innovation," *European Journal of Work and Organizational Psychology* (EJWOP), vol. 5, no. 1 (1996), pp. 105-123.
2. Ekvall, pp. 105-123.
3. Ekvall, pp. 105-123.
4. Ekvall, pp. 105-123.
5. Peter Pellegrino, from a personal conversation, December 1995. Used by permission.
6. Pellegrino.
7. Pellegrino.
8. Dick Richards, *Artful Work* (San Francisco, Calif.: Benett-Koehler Publishers, 1995), pp. 46-48.

Author

DR. ROGER L. FIRESTIEN is president of Innovation Resources, Inc and associate professor at the International Center for Studies in Creativity at Buffalo State College in Buffalo, New York.

Internationally acclaimed speaker, author, and consultant, Dr. Firestien has designed and presented programs in Creative Problem Solving to thousands of people in audiences throughout the United States, Europe, and South America. His interactive programs ignite personal and group creativity.

Dr. Firestien is the author of more than seventy articles, books, and audio or video programs published in both the popular and professional press. Some of his publications include: *From Basics to Breakthroughs, Power Think,* and the creativity fable *Why Didn't I Think of That?* He is the host and author of the video program, *Unleashing the Power of Creativity: The Key to Teamwork, Empowerment and Continuous Improvement.*

His expert views on creativity have been reported in *Training Magazine, Young Executive, Entrepreneur, Success Magazine, Self Magazine,* and *Delta Airlines SKY Magazine.*

As a speaker and seminar leader, Dr. Firestien has been described as "having a Midas touch" with audiences. His seminars have been dubbed "powerfully positive performances" and "100 percent outstanding."

Dr. Firestien holds a Bachelor of Arts degree from the University of Northern Colorado, a Master of Science degree in Creative Studies from Buffalo State College, and the Doctor of Philosophy degree in Communication from the State University of New York at Buffalo.